TREASURES OF
THE ALHAMBRA

TEXT: **WASHINGTON IRVING**
FOREWORD: **LUDWING VON HALLE**
DESIGN: **J. OPISSO**
PHOTOGRAPHS: **F. MONFORT**

1st. Edition, March 1979
I.S.B.N.
84-7424-085-9

TREASURES OF THE ALHAMBRA

Traveling in groups is not a modern day invention. From ancient times nomadic people traveled in groups and large periodical movements: migrations, exodus, pilgrimages, etc. These groups, impelled by famine or wars, were not, obviously, familiar with the serene art of traveling. The word "tourist" was first used in our century by the great British traveler D.H. Lawrence: the word is already a forerunner of social and mass tourism.

In the midst of the crowded touristic boom, the old-fashioned traveler longingly remembers the times when traveling around the world was still an adventure. When it was not just a sociologic need, or a way to study geography: it was an art, a pleasure for the senses as well as nourishment for the fancy.

When Montaigne tells about his trip to the bathing resort of Plombieres he does not mention the cathedrals or monuments that he encounters on his way. He admires the landscape, the silverware at the hotels, the squares in the towns... passing up the Gothic churches altogether. The diary of a traveler accepts, however, all kinds of commentators: from the philosophical itinerary of Montaigne, to the memoires of Casanova, or the psicological monologue of George Sand. The most influential writers in their time were great travelers: Rousseau, Voltaire, Byron, Lamartine, Hemingway...

The American chronicler and narrator Washington Irving can also be included in this list of illustrious traveling writers. His book "Tales of the Alhambra" is an authentic diary of a journey, where history and legend are blended with living journalism and imagination. The Spain he met early in the 19th century was also a mixture of history, legend, wit, and romanticism. His skillful pen was able to discover and describe all the secrets hidden in the old Arabic palaces of Granada, recovering the lost history from their darkest corners.

To travel is an art. To write a good traveling book is twice that art. The publishers wish to add a new aesthetic pleasure to this collection of Washington Irving's tales: a varied, beautiful photographic illustration.

Lydia Beltrán

Partial view of Granada in the neighborhood of
Albaicin.

Carrera del Darro.

The Alcazaba as seen from the Albaicin.

Narrow street of the Albaicin.

PALACE OF THE ALHAMBRA

To the traveller imbued with a feeling for the historical and poetical, so inseparately interwined in the annals of romantic Spain, the Alhambra is as much an object of devotion as is the Caaba to all true Moslems. How many legends and traditions, true and fabulous, —how many songs and ballads, Arabian and Spanish, of love and war and chivalry, are associated with this Oriental pile! It was the royal abode of the Moorish kings, where, surrounded with the splendours and refinements of Asiatic luxury, they held dominion over what they vaunted as a terrestrial paradise, and made their last stand for empire in Spain. The royal palace forms but a part of a fortress, the walls of which, studded with towers, stretch irregularly round the whole crest of a hill, a spur of the Sierra Nevada or Snowy Mountains, and overlook the city; externally it is a rude congregation of towers and battlements, with no regularity of plan nor grace of architecture, and giving little promise of the grace and beauty which prevail within.

In the time of the Moors the fortress was capable of containing within its outward precincts an army of forty thousand men, and served occasionally as a stronghold of the sovereigns against their rebellious subjects. After the kingdom had passed into the hands of the Christians, the Alhambra continued to be a royal demesne, and was occasionally inhabited by the Castilian monarchs. The emperor Charles V. commenced a sumptuous palace within its walls, but was deterred from completing it by repeated shocks of earthquakes. The last royal residents were Philip V. and his beautiful queen, Elizabetta of Parma, early in the eighteenth century. Great preparations were made for their reception. The palace and gardens were placed in a state of repair, and a new suite of apartments erected, and decorated by artists brought from Italy. The sojourn of the sovereigns was transient, and after their departure the palace once more became desolate. Still the place was maintained with some military state. The governor held it immediately from the crown, its jurisdiction extended down into the suburbs of the city, and was independent of the captain-general of Granada. A considerable garrison was kept up; the governor had his apartments in the front of the old Moorish palace, and never descended into Granada without some military parade. The fortress, in fact, was a little town of itself, having several streets of houses within its walls, together with a Franciscan convent and a parochial church.

The desertion of the court, however, was a fatal blow to the Alhambra. Its beautiful halls became desolate, and some of them fell to ruin; the gardens were destroyed, and the fountains ceased to play. By degrees the dwellings became filled with a loose and lawless population: **contrabandistas,** who availed themselves of its independent jurisdiction to carry on a wide and daring course of smuggling, and thieves and rogues of all sorts, who made this their palace of refuge whence they might depredate upon Granada and its vicinity. The strong arm of government at length interfered; the whole community was thoroughly sifted; none were suffered to remain but such as were of honest character, and had legitimate right to a residence; the greater part of the houses were demolished and a mere hamlet left, with the parochial church and the Franciscan convent. During the recent troubles in Spain, when Granada was in the hands of the French, the Alhambra was garrisoned by their troops, and the palace was occasionally inhabited by the French commander. With that enlightened taste which has ever distinguished the French nation in their conquests, this monument of Moorish elegance and grandeur was rescued from the absolute ruin and desolation that were overwhelming it. The roofs were repaired, the saloons and galleries protected from the weather, the gardens cultivated, the watercourses restored, the fountains once more made to throw up their sparkling showers; and Spain may thank her invaders for having preserved to her the most beautiful and interesting of her historical monuments.

On the departure of the French they blew up several towers of the outer wall, and left the fortifications scarcely tenable. Since that time the military importance of the post is at an end. The garrison is a handful of invalid soldiers, whose principal duty is to guard some of the outer towers, which serve occasionally as a prison of state; and the governor, abandoning the lofty hill of the Alhambra, resides in the centre of Granada, for the more convenient despatch of his official duties.

Our first object of course, on the morning after our arrival, was a visit to this time-honoured edifice; it has been so often, however, and so

Different views of the neighborhood of the Albaicin.

Geraniums, forged iron balconies, "Carmenes" (courtyards), and Moorish architecture.

minutely described by travellers, that I shall not undertake to give a comprehensive and elaborate account of it, but merely occasional sketches of parts, with the incidents and associations connected with them.

Leaving our **posada,** and traversing the renowned square of the Vivarrambla, once the scene of Moorish jousts and tournaments, now a crowded market-place, we proceeded along the Zacatin, the main street of what, in the time of the Moors, was the Great Bazaar, and where small shops and narrow alleys still retain the Oriental character. Crossing an open place in front of the palace of the captain-general, we ascended a confined and winding street, the name of which reminded us of the chivalric days of Granada. It is called the Calle, or street of the Gomeres, from a Moorish family famous in chronicle and song. This street led up to the Puerta de las Granadas, a massive gateway of Grecian architecture, built by Charles V., forming the entrance to the domains of the Alhambra.

At the gate were two or three ragged superannuated soldiers, dozing on a stone bench, the successors of the Zegris and the Abencerrages; while a tall meagre varlet, whose rusty-brown cloak was evidently intented to conceal the ragged state of his nether garments, was lounging in the sunshine and gossiping with an ancient sentinel on duty. He joined us as we entered the gate, and offered his services to show us the fortress.

I have a traveller's dislike to officious ciceroni, and did not altogether like the garb of the applicant.

«You are well acquainted with the place, I presume?»

«Ninguno más; pues señor, soy hijo de la Alhambra».

(Nobody better; in fact, sir, I am a son of the Alhambra!)

The common Spaniards have certainly a most poetical way of expressing themselves. «A son of the Alhambra»! the appellation caught me at once; the very tattered garb of my new acquaintance assumed a dignity in my eyes. It

was emblematic of the fortunes of the place, and befitted the progeny of a ruin.

I put some further questions to him, and found that his title was legitimate. His family had lived in the fortress from generation to generation ever since the time of the Conquest. His name was Mateo Ximenes. «Then, perhaps», said I, «you may be a descendant from the great Cardinal Ximenes?» **—Dios sabe!** God knows, Señor! It may be so. We are the oldest family in the Alhambra, **—Christianos viejos,** old Christians, without any taint of Moor or Jew. I know we belong to some great family or other, but I forgot whom. My father knows all about it: he has the coat of arms hanging up in his cottage, up in the fortress». There is not any Spaniard, however poor, but has some claim to high pedigree. The first tittle of this ragged worthy, however, had completely captivated me; so I gladly accepted the services of the «son of the Alhambra».

We now found ourselves in a deep narrow ravine, filled with beautiful groves, with a steep avenue, and various footpaths winding through it, bordered with stone seats, and ornamented with fountains. To our left we beheld the towers of the Alhambra beetling above us; to our right, on the opposite side of the ravine, we were equally dominated by rival towers on a rocky eminence. These, we were told, were the Torres Vermejos, or vermilion towers, so called from their ruddy hue.

No one knows their origin. They are of a date much anterior to the Alhambra: some suppose them to have been built by the Romans; others, by some wandering colony of Phœnicians. Ascending the steep and shady avenue, we arrived at the foot of a huge square Moorish tower, forming a kind of barbican, through which passed the main entrance to the fortress. Within the barbican was another group of veteran invalids, one mounting guard at the portal, while the rest, wrapped in their tattered cloaks, slept on the stone benches. This portal is called the Gate of Justice, from the tribunal held within its porch during the Moslem domination, for the immediate trial of petty causes: a custom

General view of
the Alhambra.

common to the Oriental nations, and occasionally alluded to in the sacred Scriptures. «Judges and officers shalt thou make thee **in all thy gates,** and they shall judge the people with just judgment».

The great vestibule, or porch of the gate is formed by an immense Arabian arch, of the horseshoe form, which springs to half the height of the tower. On the keystone of this arch is engraven a gigantic hand. Within the vestibule, on the keystone of the portal, is sculptured, in like manner, a gigantic key. Those who pretend to some knowledge of Mohammedan symbols, affirm that the hand is the emblem of doctrine; the five fingers designating the five principal commandments of the creed of Islam, fasting, pilgrimage, alms-giving, ablution, and war against infidels. The key, say they, is the emblem of the faith or of power; the key of Daoud, or David, transmitted to the prophet. «And the key of the house of David will I lay upon his shoulder; so he shall open, and none shall shut, and he shall shut, and none shall open». (Isaiah xxii, 22) The key we are told was emblazoned on the standard of the Moslems in opposition to the Christian emblem of the cross, when they subdued Spain or Andalusia. It betokened the conquering power invested in the prophet. «He that hath the key of David, he that openeth, and no man shutteth; and shutteth, and no man openeth». (Rev. iii. 7.)

A different explanation of these emblems, however, was given by the legitimate son of the Alhambra, and one more in unison with the notions of the common people, who attach something of mystery and magic to everything Moorish, and have all kinds of superstitions connected with this old Moslem fortress. According to Mateo, it was a tradition handed down from the oldest inhabitants, and which he had from his father and grandfather, that the hand and key were magical devices on which the fate of the Alhambra depended. The Moorish king who built it was a great magician, or, as some believed, had sold himself to the devil, and had laid the whole fortress under a magic spell. By this means it had remained

standing, for several years, in defiance of storms and earthquakes, while almost all other buildings of the Moors had fallen to ruin and disappeared. This spell, the tradition went on to say, would last until the hand on the outer arch should reach down and grasp the key, when the whole pile would tumble to pieces, and all the treasures buried beneath it by the Moors would be revealed.

Notwithstanding this ominous prediction, we ventured to pass through the spell-bound gateway, feeling some little assurance against magic art in the protection of the Virgin, a statue of whom we observed above the portal.

After passing through the barbican, we ascended a narrow lane, winding between walls, and came on an open esplanade within the fortress called the Plaza de los Algibes, or Place of the Cisterns, from great reservoirs which undermine it, cut in the living rock by the Moors to receive the water brought by conduits from the Darro, for the supply of the fortress. Here, also, is a well of immense depth, furnishing the purest and coldest of water, —another monument of the delicate taste of the Moors, who were indefatigable in their exertions to obtain that element in its crystal purity.

In front of this esplanade is the splendid pile commenced by Charles V., and intended, it is said, to eclipse the residence of the Moorish kings. Much of the Oriental edifice intended for the winter season was demolished to make way for this massive pile. The grand entrance was blocked up; so that the present entrance to the Moorish palace is through a simple and almost humble portal in a corner. With all the massive grandeur and architectural merit of the palace of Charles V., we regarded it as an arrogant intruder, and passing by it with a feeling almost of scorn, rang at the Moslem portal.

While waiting for admittance, our self-imposed cicerone, Mateo Ximenes, informed us that the royal palace was intrusted to the care of a worthy old maiden dame called Doña Antonia Molina, but who, according to Spanish custom, went by the more neighbourly appelation of Tía Antonia (Aunt Antonia), who maintained the

Moorish halls and gardens in order and showed them to strangers. While we were talking the door was opened by a plump little black-eyed Andalusian damsel, whom Mateo addressed as Dolores, but who from her bright looks and cheerful disposition evidently merited a merrier name. Mateo informed me in a whisper that she was the niece of Tía Antonia, and I found she was the good fairy who was to conduct us through the enchanted palace. Under her guidance we crossed the threshold, and were at once transported, as if by magic wand, into other times and an oriental realm, and were treading the scenes of Arabian story. Nothing could be in greater contrast that the unpromising exterior of the pile with the scene now before us. We found ourselves in a vast **patio** or court, one hundred and fifty feet in length, and upwards of eighty feet in breadth, paved with white marble, and decorated at each end with light Moorish peristyles, one of which supported an elegant gallery of fretted architecture.

Along the moulding of the cornices and on various parts of the walls were escutcheons and ciphers, and cufic and Arabic characters in high relief, repeating the pious mottoes of the Moslem monarchs, the builders of the Alhambra, or extolling their grandeur and munificence. Along the centre of the court extended an immense basin or tank (**estanque**), a hundred and twenty-four feet in length,

twenty-seven in breadth, and five in depth, receiving its water from two marble vases. Hence it is called the Court of the Alberca (from **al beerkah,** the Arabic, for a pond or tank). Great numbers of gold-fish were to be seen gleaming through the waters of the basin, and it was bordered by hedges of roses.

Passing from the court of the Alberca under a Moorish archway, we entered the renowned court of Lions. No part of the edifice gives a more complete idea of its original beauty than this, for none has suffered so little from the ravages of time. In the centre stands the fountain famous in song and story. The alabaster basins still shed their diamond drops; the twelve lions which support them, and give the court its name, still cast forth crystal streams as in the days of Boabdil. The lions, however, are unworthy of their fame, being of miserable sculpture, the work probably of some Christian captive. The court is laid out in flower-beds, instead of its ancient and appropriate pavement of tiles or marble; the alteration, an instance of bad taste was made by the French when in possession of Granada. Round the four sides of the court are light Arabian arcades of open filigree work, supported by slender pillars of white marble, which it is supposed were originally gilded. The architecture, like that in most parts of the interior of the palace, is characterised by elegance rather than grandeur,

Different scenes from the Alhambra.

bespeaking a delicate and graceful taste, and a disposition to indolent enjoyment. When one looks upon the fairy traces of the peristyles, and the apparently fragile fretwork of the walls, it is difficult to believe that so much has survived the wear and tear of centuries, the shocks of earthquakes, the violence of war, and the quiet, through no less baneful, pilferings of the tasteful traveller: it is almost sufficient to excuse the popular tradition, that the whole is protected by a magic charm.

On one side of the court a rich portal opens into the Hall of the Abencerrages: so called from the gallant cavaliers of that illustrious line who were here perfidiously massacred. There are some who doubt the whole story, but our humble cicerone Mateo pointed out the very wicket of the portal through which they were introduced one by one into the court of Lions, and the white marble fountain in the centre of the hall beside which they were beheaded. He showed us also certain broad ruddy stains on the pavement, traces of their blood, which, according to popular belief, can never be effaced.

Finding we listened to him apparently with easy faith, he added, that there was often heard at night, in the court of Lions, a low confused sound, resembling the murmuring of a multitude, and now and then a faint tinkling, like the distant clank of chains. These sounds

were made by the spirits of the murdered Abencerrages, who nightly haunt the scene of their suffering and invoke the vengeance of Heaven on their destroyer.

The sounds in question had no doubt been produced, as I had afterwards an opportunity of ascertaining, by the bubbling currents and tinkling falls of water conducted under the pavement through pipes and channels to supply the fountains; but I was too considerate to intimate such an idea to the humble chronicler of the Alhambra.

Encouraged by my easy credulity, Mateo gave me the following as an undoubted fact, which he had from his grandfather: —

There was once an invalid soldier, who had charge of the Alhambra to show it to strangers; as he was one evening, about twilight, passing through the court of Lions, he heard footsteps on the hall of the Abencerrages; supposing some strangers to be lingering there, he advanced to attend upon them, when to his astonishment he beheld four Moors richly dressed, with gilded cuirasses and cimeters, and poniards glittering with precious stones. They were walking to and fro, with solemn pace; but paused and beckoned to him. The old soldier, however, took to flight, and could never afterwards be prevailed upon to enter the Alhambra. Thus it is that men sometimes turn their backs upon fortune; for it is the firm opinion of Mateo, that the Moors intended to reveal the place where their treasures lay buried. A successor to the invalid soldier was more knowing; he came to the Alhambra poor; but at the end of a year went off to Malaga, bought houses, set up a carriage, and still lives there, one of the richest as well as oldest men of the place; all which, Mateo sagely surmised, was in consequence of his finding out the golden secret of these phantom Moors.

I now perceived I had made an invaluable acquaintance in this son of the Alhambra, one who knew all the apocryphal history of the place and firmly believed in it, and whose memory was stuffed with a kind of knowledge for which I have a lurking fancy, but which is too apt to be considered rubbish by less indulgent philosophers. I determined to cultivate the acquaintance of this learned Theban. Immediately opposite the hall of the Abencerrages, a portal, richly adorned, leads into a hall of less tragical associations. It is light and lofty, exquisitely graceful in its architecture, paved with marble, and bears the suggestive name of the Hall of the Two Sisters. Some destroy the romance of the name by attributing it to two enormous slabs of alabaster which lie side by side, and form a great part of the pavement: an opinion strongly supported by Mateo Ximenes. Others are disposed to give the name a more poetical significance, as the vague memorial of Moorish beauties who once graced this hall, which was evidently a part of the royal harem. This opinion I was happy to find entertained by our little bright-eyed guide, Dolores, who pointed to a balcony over an inner porch, which gallery, she had been told, belonged to the women's apartment. «You see, **señor,»** said she, «it is all grated and latticed, like the gallery in a convent chapel where the nuns hear mass; for the Moorish kings,» added she, indignantly, «shut up their wives just like nuns».

The latticed **jalousies,** in fact, still remain, whence the dark-eyed beauties of the harem might gaze unseen upon the **zambras** and other dances and entertainments of the hall below. On each side of this hall are recesses or alcoves for ottomans and couches, on which the voluptuous lords of the Alhambra indulged in that dreamy repose so dear to the Orientalists. A cupola or lantern admits a tempered light from above and a free circulation of air; while on one side is heard the refreshing sound of waters from the fountain of the lions, and on the other side the soft plash from the basin in the garden of Lindaraxa.

It is impossible to contemplate this scene, so perfectly Oriental, without feeling the early associations of Arabian romance, and almost expecting to see the white arm of some mysterious princess beckoning from the gallery, or some dark eye sparkling through the lattice.

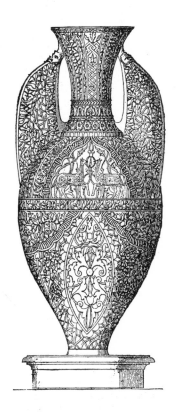

The abode of beauty is here as if it had been inhabited but yesterday; but where are the two sisters, where the Zoraydas and Lindaraxas! An abundant supply of water, brought from the mountains by old Moorish aqueducts, circulates throughout the palace, supplying its baths and fish-pools, sparkling in jets within its halls or murmuring in channels along the marble pavements. When it has paid its tribute to the royal pile, and visited its gardens and parterres, it flows down the long avenue leading to the city, tinkling in rills, gushing in fountains, and maintaining a perpetual verdure in those groves that embower and beautify the whole hill of the Alhambra.

Those only who have sojourned in the ardent climates of the South can appreciate the delights of an abode combining the breezy coolness of the mountain with the freshness and verdure of the valley. While the city below pants with the moontide heat, and the parched Vega trembles to the eye, the delicate airs from the Sierra Nevada play through these lofty halls, bringing

The Alhambra
as seen from
El Generalife.

Sunset at the
Alhambra.

with them the sweetness of the surrounding gardens. Everything invites to that indolent repose, the bliss of southern climes; and while the half-shut eye looks out from shaded balconies upon the glittering landscape, the ear is lulled by the rustling of groves and the murmur of running streams.

I forbear for the present, however, to describe the other delightful apartments of the palace. My object is merely to give the reader a general introduction into an abode where, if so disposed, he may linger and loiter with me day by day until we gradually become familiar with all its localities.

THE HALL OF AMBASSADORS

In one of my visits to the old Moorish chamber where the good Tia Antonia cooks her dinner and receives her company, I observed a mysterious door in one corner, leading apparently into the ancient part of the edifice. My curiosity being aroused, I opened it, and found myself in a narrow, blind corridor, groping along which I came to the head of a dark winding staircase, leading down an angle of the tower of Comares. Down this staircase I descended darkling, guiding myself by the wall until I came to a small door at the bottom, throwing which open, I was suddenly dazzled by emerging into the brilliant antechamber of the Hall of Ambassadors; with the fountain of the court of the Alberca sparkling before me. The antechamber is separated with the court by an elegant gallery, supported by slender columns with spandrels of openwork in the Morisco style. At each end of the antechamber are alcoves, and its ceiling is richly stuccoed and painted. Passing through a magnificent portal, I found myself in the far-famed Hall of Ambassadors, the audience chamber of the Moslem monarchs. It is said to be thirty-seven feet square, and sixty feet high; occupies the whole interior of the Tower of Comares; and still bears the traces of past magnificence. The walls are beautifully stuccoed and decorated with Morisco fancifulness; the lofty ceiling was originally of the same favourite material, with the usual frostwork and pensile ornaments or stalactites; which. with the embellishments of vivid colouring and gilding, must have been gorgeous in the extreme. Unfortunately it gave way during an earthquake, and brought down with it an immense arch which traversed the hall. It was replaced by the present vault or dome of larch or cedar, with intersecting ribs, the whole curiously wrought and richly coloured; still Oriental in its character, reminding one of «those ceilings of cedar and vermilion that we read of in the Prophets and the **Arabian Nights**».[1]

From the great height of the vault above the windows, the upper part of the hall is almost lost in obscurity; yet there is a magnificence as well as solemnity in the gloom, as through it we have gleams of rich gilding and the brilliant tints of the Moorish pencil.

The royal throne was placed opposite the entrance in a recess, which still bears an inscription intimating that Yusef I (the monarch who completed the Alhambra) made this the throne of his empire. Everything in this noble hall seems to have been calculated to surround the throne with impressive dignity and splendour; there was none of the elegant voluptuousness which reigns in other parts of the palace. The tower is of massive strength, domineering over the whole edifice and overhanging the steep hillside. On three sides of the Hall of Ambassadors are windows cut through the immense thickness of the walls and commanding extensive prospects. The balcony of the central window especially looks down upon the verdant valley of the Darro, with its walks, its groves, and gardens. To the left it enjoys a distant prospect of the Vega; while directly in front rises the rival height of the Albaycin, with its medley of streets, and terraces, and gardens, and once crowned by a fortress that vied in power with the Alhambra. «Ill fated the man who lost all this!» exclaimed Charles V., as he looked forth from this window upon the enchanting scenery it commands. The balcony of the window where this royal exclamation was made, has of late become one

[1] Urquhart's **Pillars of Hercules**.

View of the Alhambra from the Carrera del Darro.

Walls of the Alcazaba.

Court of the Alcazaba.

of my favourite resorts. I have just been seated there, enjoying the close of a brilliant long day. The sun, as he sank behind the purple mountains of Alhama, sent a stream of effulgence up the valley of the Darro, that spread a melancholy pomp over the ruddy towers of the Alhambra; while the Vega, covered with a slight sultry vapour that caught the setting ray, seemed spread out in the distance like a golden sea. Not a breath of air disturbed the stillness of the hour, and though the faint sound of music and merriment now and then rose from the gardens of the Darro, it but rendered more impressive the monumental silence of the pile which overshadowed me. It was one of those hours and scenes in which memory asserts an almost magical power: and, like the evening sun beaming on these mouldering towers, sends back her retrospective rays to light up the glories of the past.

As I sat watching the effect of the declining daylight upon this Moorish pile, I was led into a consideration of the light, elegant, and voluptuous character prevalent throughout its internal architecture, and to contrast it with the grand but gloomy solemnity of the Gothic edifices reared by the Spanish conquerors. The very architecture thus bespeaks the opposite and irreconcilable natures of the two warlike people who so long battled here for the mastery of the Peninsula. By degrees I fell into a course of musing upon the singular fortunes of the Arabian or Morisco-Spaniards, whose whole existence is as a tale that is told, and certainly forms one of the most anomalous yet splendid episodes in history. Potent and durable as was their dominion, we scarcely know how to call them. They were a nation without a legitimate country or name. A remote wave of the great Arabian inundation, cast upon the shores of Europe, they seem to have all the impetus of the first rush of the torrent. Their career of conquest, from the rock of Gibraltar, to the cliffs of the Pyrenees, was as rapid and brilliant as the Moslem victories of Syria and Egypt. Nay, had they not been checked on the plains of Tours, all France, all Europe, might have been overrun

with the same facility as the empires of the East, and the Crescent at this day have glittered on the fanes of Paris and London.

Repelled within the limits of the Pyrenees, the mixed hordes of Asia and Africa, that formed this great irruption, gave up the Moslem principle of conquest, and sought to establish in Spain a peaceful and permanent dominion. As conquerors, their heroism was only equalled by their moderation; and in both, for a time, they excelled the nations with whom they contended. Severed from their native homes, they loved the land given them as they supposed by Allah, and strove to embellish it with everything that could administer to the happiness of man. Laying the foundations of their power in a system of wise and equitable laws, diligently cultivating the arts and sciences, and promoting agriculture, manufactures, and commerce, they gradually formed an empire unrivalled for its prosperity by any of the empires of Christendom; and diligently drawing round them the graces and refinements which marked the Arabian empire in the East, at the time of its greatest civilisation, they diffused the light of Oriental knowledge through the western regions of benighted Europe.

The cities of Arabian Spain became the resort of Christian artisans, to instruct themselves in the useful arts. The universities of Toledo, Cordoba, Seville, and Granada were sought by the pale student from other lands to acquaint himself with the sciences of the Arabs and the treasured lore of antiquity; the lovers of the gay science resorted to Cordova and Granada, to imbibe the poetry and music of the East; and the steel-clad warriors of the North hastened thither to accomplish themselves in the graceful exercises and courteous usages of chivalry.

If the Moslem monuments in Spain, if the Mosque of Cordova, the Alcazar of Seville, and the Alhambra of Granada, still bear inscriptions fondly boasting of the power and permanency of their dominion, can the boast be derided as arrogant and vain? Generation after generation, century after century, passed away, and still they maintained posession of the land. A period elapsed longer than that which has passed since England was subjugated by the Norman Conqueror, and the descendants of Musa and Taric might as little anticipate being driven into exile across the same straits, traversed by their triumphant ancestors, as the descendants of Rollo and William, and their veteran peers, may dream of being driven back to the shores of Normandy.

With all this, however, the Moslem empire in Spain was but a brilliant exotic, that took no permanent root in the soil it embellished. Severed from all their neighbours in the West by impassable barriers of faith and manners, and separated by seas and deserts from their kindred of the East, the Morisco-Spaniards were an isolated people. Their whole existence was a prolonged, though gallant and chivalric struggle for a foothold in a usurped land.

They were the outposts and frontiers of Islamism. The Peninsula was the great battle-ground where the Gothic conquerors of the North and the Moslem conquerors of the East met and strove for mastery; and the fiery courage of the Arab was at length subdued by the obstinate and persevering valour of the Goth.

Never was the annihilation of a people more complete than that of the Morisco-Spaniards. Where are they? Ask the shores of Barnaby and its desert places. The exiled remnant of their once powerful empire disappeared among the barbarians of Africa, and ceased to be a nation. They have not even left a distinct name behind

Gate of Justice.

Wall fountain of
Carlos V.

Fountain of
Carlos V (detail).

Night view of the Puerta del Vino (Wine Gate).

Polychromed tiles and twin balconies at the Puerta
del Vino.

them, though for nearly eight centuries they were a distinct people. The home of their adoption, and of their occupation for ages, refuses to acknowledge them, except as invaders and usurpers. A few broken monuments are all that remain to bear witness to their power and dominion, as solitary rocks, left far in the interior, bear testimony to the extent of some vast inundation. Such is the Alhambra;—a Moslem pile in the midst of a Christian land; an Oriental palace amidst the Gothic edifices of the West; an elegant memento of a brave, intelligent, and graceful people, who conquered, ruled, flourished, and passed away.

THE MYSTERIOUS CHAMBERS

As I was rambling one day about the Moorish halls, my attention was, for the first time, attracted to a door in a remote gallery, communicating apparently with some part of the Alhambra which I had not yet explored. I attempted to open it, but it was locked. I knocked, but no one answered, and the sound seemed to reverberate through empty chambers. Here then was a mystery. Here was the haunted wing of the castle. How was I to get at the dark secrets here shut up from the public eye? Should I come privately at night with lamp and sword, according to the prying custom of heroes of romance; or should I endeavour to draw the secret from Pépe the stuttering gardener; or the ingenuous Dolores, or the loquacious Mateo? Or should I go frankly and openly to Dame Antonia the chatelaine, and ask her all about it? I chose the latter course, as being the simplest though the least romantic; and found, somewhat to my disappointment, that there was no mystery in the case. I was welcome to explore the apartment, and there was the key.

Thus provided, I returned forthwith to the door. It opened, as I had surmised, to a range of vacant chambers; but they were quite different from the rest of the palace. The architecture, though rich and antiquated, was European. There was nothing Moorish about it. The first two rooms were lofty; the ceilings, broken in many places, were of cedar, deeply panelled and skilfully carved with fruits and flowers, intermingled with grotesque masks or faces. The walls had evidently in ancient times been hung with damask; but now were naked, and scrawled over by that class of aspiring travellers who defile noble monuments with their worthless names. The windows, dismantled and open to wind and weather, looked out into a charming little secluded garden, where an alabaster fountain sparkled among roses and myrtles, and was surrounded by orange and citron trees, some of which flung their branches into the chambers. Beyond these rooms were two saloons, longer but less lofty, looking also into the garden. In the compartments of the panelled ceilings were baskets of fruit and garlands of flowers, painted by no mean hand, and in tolerable preservation. The walls also had been painted in fresco in the Italian style, but the paintings were nearly obliterated; the windows were in the same shattered state with those of the other chambers. This fanciful suite of rooms terminated in an open gallery with balustrades, runnind at right angles along another side of the garden. The whole apartment, so delicate and elegant in its decorations, so choice and sequestered in its situation along this retired little garden, and so different in architecture from the neighbouring halls, awakened an interest in its history. I found on inquiry that it was an apartment fitted up by Italian artists in the early part of the last century, at the time when Philip V. and his second wife, the beautiful Elizabetta of Farnese, daughter of the Duke of Parma, were expected at the Alhambra. It was destined for the queen and the ladies of her train. One of the loftiest chambers had been her sleeping-room. A narrow staircase, now walled up, led up to a delightful belvidere, originally a mirador of the Moorish sultanas, communicating with the harem; but which was fitted up as a boudoir for the fair Elizabetta, and still retains the name of **el tocador de la Reyna,** or the queen's toilette.

One window of the royal sleeping-room commanded a prospect of the Generalife and its

embowered terraces; another looked out into the little secluded garden I have mentioned, which was decidedly Moorish in its character, and also had its history. It was in fact the garden of Lindaraxa, so often mentioned in descriptions of the Alhambra, but who this Lindaraxa was I had never heard explained. A little research gave me the few particulars known about her. She was a Moorish beauty who flourished in the court of Muhamed the Left-Handed, and was the daughter of his royal adherent, the **alcayde** of Málaga, who sheltered him in his city when driven from the throne. On regaining his crown, the **alcayde** was rewarded for his fidelity. His daughter had her apartment in the Alhambra, and was given by the king in marriage to Nasar, a young Cetimerien prince descended from Aben Hud the Just. Their espousals, were doubtless celebrated in the royal palace and their honeymoon may have passed among these very bowers![1]

Four centuries had elapsed since the fair Lindaraxa passed away, yet how much of the fragile beauty of the scenes she inhabited remained! The garden still bloomed in which she delighted; the fountain still presented the crystal mirror in which her charms may once have been reflected; the alabaster, it is true, had lost its whiteness; the basin beneath, overrun with weeds, had become the lurking-place of the lizard, but there was something in the very decay that enhanced the interest of the scene, speaking as it did of that mutability, the irrevocable lot of man and all his works.

The desolation too of these chambers, once the abode of the proud and elegant Elizabetta, had a more touching charm for me than if I had beheld them in their pristine splendour, glittering with the pageantry of a court.

When I returned to my quarters in the

1.
One of the things in which the Moorish kings interfered was in the marriage of their nobles: hence it came that all the señors attached to the royal person were married in the palace; and there was always a chamber destined for the ceremony.—**Paseo por Granada**, Paseo XXI.

Panoramic view and details of the Arrayanes Court.

governor's apartment, everything seemed tame and commonplace after the poetic region I had left. The thought suggested itself: Why could I not change my quarters to these vacant chambers? that would indeed be living in the Alhambra, surrounded by its gardens and fountains, an in the time of the Moorish sovereigns. I proposed the change to Dame Antonia and her family, and it occasioned vast surprise. They could not conceive any rational inducement for the choice of an apartment so forlorn, remote, and solitary. Dolores exclaimed at its frightful loneliness; nothing but bats and owls flitting about,—and then a fox and wildcat, kept in the vaults of the neighbouring baths, roamed about at night. The good Tía had more reasonable objections. The neighbourhood was infested by vagrants: gipsies swarmed in the caverns of the adjacent hills; the palace was ruinous and easy to be entered in many places; the rumour of a stranger quartered alone in one of the remote and ruined apartments, out of the hearing of the rest of the inhabitants, might tempt unwelcome visitors in the night, especially as foreigners were always supposed to be well stocked with money. I was not to be diverted from my humour, however, and my will was law with these good people. So, calling in the assistance of a carpenter, and the ever officious Mateo Ximenes, the doors and windows were soon placed in a state of tolerable security, and the sleeping-room of the stately Elizabetta prepared for my reception. Mateo kindly volunteered as a body-guard to sleep in my antechamber; but I did not think it worth while to put his valour to the proof.

With all the hardihood I had assumed and all the precautions I had taken, I must confess the first night passed in these quarters was inexpressibly dreary. I do not think it was so much the apprehension of dangers from without that affected me, as the character of the place itself, with all its strange associations: the deeds of violence committed there; the tragical ends of many of those who had once reigned there in splendour. As I passed beneath the fated halls of the tower of Comares on the way to my chamber, I called to mind a quotation that used to thrill me in the days of boyhood:

«Fate sits on these dark battlements and frowns;
And, as the portal opens to receive me,
A voice in sullen echoes through the courts
Tells of a nameless deed!»

The whole family escorted me to my chamber, and took leave of me as of one engaged in a perilous enterprise; and when I heard their retreating steps die away along the waste antechambers and echoing galleries, and turned the key of my door, I was reminded of those hobgoblin stories, where the hero is left to accomplish the adventure of an enchanted house.

Even the thoughts of the fair Elizabetta and the beauties of her court, who had once graced these chambers, now, by a perversion of fancy, added to the gloom. Here was the scene of their transient gaiety and loveliness; here were the very traces of their elegance and enjoyment; but what and where were they? Dust and ashes! tenants of the tomb! phantoms of the memory! A vague and indescribable awe was creeping over me. I would fain have ascribed it to the thoughts of robbers awakened by the evening's conversation, but I felt it was something more unreal and absurd. The long-buried superstitions of the nursery were reviving, and asserting their power over my imagination. Everything began to be affected by the working of my mind. The whispering of the wind among the citron-trees beneath my window had something sinister. I cast my eyes into the garden of Lindaraxa; the groves presented a gulf of shadows; the thickets, indistinct and ghastly shapes. I was glad to close the window, but my chamber itself became infected. There was a slight rustling noise overhead; a bat suddenly emerged from a broken panel of the ceiling, flitting about the room and athwart my solitary lamp; and as the fateful bird almost flouted my face with his noiseless wing, the grotesque faces carved in high relief in the cedar ceiling, whence he had emerged, seemed to mope and mow at me.

Rousing myself, and half smiling at this temporary weakness, I resolved to brave it out in the true spirit of the hero of the enchanted

Tiles, "atauriques" (Moorish plaster works), lattice works, and "mocárabes" (arch-shaped ornaments) decorating the walls of the Alhambra.

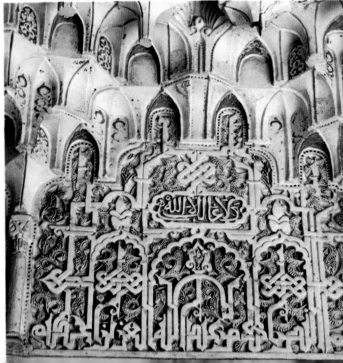

house; so, taking lamp in hand, I sallied forth to make a tour of the palace. Notwithstanding every mental exertion the task was a severe one. I had to traverse waste halls and mysterious galleries, where the rays of the lamp extended but a short distance around me. I walked, as it were, in a mere halo of light, walled in by impenetrable darkness. The vaulted corridors were as caverns; the ceilings of the halls were lost in gloom. I recalled all that had been said of the danger from interlopers in these remote and ruined apartments. Might not some vagrant foe be lurking before or behind me, in the outer darkness? My own shadow, cast upon the wall, began to disturb me. The echoes of my own footsteps along the corridors made me pause and look around. I was traversing scenes fraught with dismal recollections. One dark passage led down to the mosque where Yusef, the Moorish monarch, the finisher of the Alhambra, had been basely murdered. In another place I trod the gallery where another monarch had been struck down by the poniard of a relative whom he had thwarted in his love.

A low murmuring sound, as of stifled voices and clanking chains, now reached me. It seemed to come from the Hall of the Abencerrages. I knew it to be the rush of water through subterranean channels, but it sounded strangely in the night, and reminded me of the dismal stories to which it had given rise.

Soon, however, my ear was assailed by sounds

too fearfully real to be the work of fancy. As I was crossing the Hall of Ambassadors, low moans and broken ejaculations rose, as it were, from beneath my feet. I paused and listened. They then appeared to be outside of the tower—then again within. Then broke forth howlings as of an animal—then stifled shrieks and inarticulate ravings. Heard in that dead hour and singular place, the effect was thrilling. I had no desire for further perambulation; but returned to my chamber with infinitely more alacrity than I had sallied forth, and drew my breath more freely when once more within its walls and the door bolted behind me. When I awoke in the morning, with the sun shining in at my window and lighting up every part of the building with his cheerful and truth-telling beams, I could scarcely recall the shadows and fancies conjured up by the gloom of the preceding night; or believe that the scenes around me, so naked and apparent, could have been clothed with such imaginary horrors.

Still, the dismal howlings and ejaculations I had heard were not ideal; they were soon accounted for, however, by my handmaid Dolores: being the ravings of a poor maniac, a brother of her aunt, who was subject to violent paraxysms, during which he was confined in a vaulted room beneath the Hall of Ambassadors.

In the course of a few evenings a thorough change took place in the scene and its associations. The moon, which when I took possession of my new apartments was invisible, gradually gained each evening upon the darkness of the night, and at length rolled in full splendour above the towers, pouring a flood of tempered light into every court and hall. The garden beneath my window, before wrapped in gloom, was gently lighted up; the orange and citron trees were tipped with silver; the fountain sparkled in the moonbeams, and even the blush of the rose was faintly visible.

I now felt the poetic merit of the Arabic inscription on the valls,—«How beauteous is this garden; where the flowers of the earth vie with the stars of heaven. What can compare with the vase of yon alabaster fountain filled with crystal

water? nothing but the moon in her fulness, shining in the midst of an unclouded sky!»

On such heavenly nights I would sit for hours at my window inhaling the sweetness of the garden and musing on the chequered fortunes of those whose history was dimly shadowed out in the elegant memorials around. Sometimes, when all was quiet, and the clock from the distant cathedral of Granada struck the midnight hour, I have sallied out on another tour and wandered over the whole building; but how different from

A sunset seen from the Hall of Ambassadors.

Mexuar Hall.

my first tour! No longer dark and mysterious; no longer peopled with shadowy foes; no longer recalling scenes of violence and murder; all was open, spacious, beautiful; everything called up pleasing and romantic fancies; Lindaraxa once more walked in her garden; the gay chivalry of Moslem Granada once more glittered about the Court of Lions! Who can do justice to a moonlight night in such a climate and such a place? The temperature of a summer midnight in Andalusia is perfectly ethereal. We seem lifted up into a purer atmosphere; we feel a serenity of soul, a buoyancy of spirits, an elasticity of frame, which render mere existence happiness. But when moonlight is added to all this, the effect is like enchantment. Under its plastic sway the Alhambra seems to regain its pristine glories. Every rent and chasm of time; every mouldering tint and weather-stain is gone; the marble resumes its original whiteness; the long colonnades brighten in the moonbeams; the halls are illuminated with a softened radiance, —we tread the enchanted palace of an Arabian tale!.

What a delight, at such a time, to ascend to the little airy pavilion of the queen's toilette (**el tocador de la reyna**), which, like a bird-cage, overhangs the valley of the Darro, and gaze from its light arcades upon the moonlight prospect! To the right, the swelling mountains of the Sierra Nevada, robbed of their ruggedness and softened into a fairy land, with their snowy summits gleaming like silver clouds against the deep blue sky. And then to lean over the parapet of the Tocador and gaze down upon Granada and the Albaycin spread out like a map below; all buried in deep repose; the white palaces and convents sleeping in the moonshine, and beyond all these the vapoury Vega fading away like a dreamland in the distance.

Sometimes the faint click of castanets rise from the Alameda, where some gay Andalusians are dancing away the summer night. Sometimes the dubious tones of a guitar and the notes of an amorous voice, tell perchance the whereabout of some moonstruck lover serenading his lady's window.

Such is a faint picture of the moonlight nights I have passed loitering about the courts and halls and balconies of this most suggestive pile; «feeding my fancy with sugared suppositions», and enjoying that mixture of reverie and sensation which steal away existence in a southern climate; so that it has been almost morning before I have retired to bed, and been lulled to sleep by the falling waters of the fountain of Lindaraxa.

THE COURT OF LIONS

The peculiar charm of this old dreamy palace is its power of calling up vague reveries and picturings of the past, and thus clothing naked realities with the illusions of the memory and the imagination. As I delight to walk in these «vain shadows», I am prone to seek those parts of the Alhambra which are most favourable to this phantasmagoria of the mind; and none are more so than the Court of Lions, and its surrounding halls. Here the hand of time has fallen the lightest, and the traces of Moorish elegance and splendour exist in almost their original brilliancy. Earthquakes have shaken the foundations of this pile, and rent its rudest towers; yet see! not one of those slender columns has been displaced, not an arch of that light and fragile colonnade given way, and all the fairy fretwork of these domes, apparently as unsubstantial as the crystal fabrics of a morning's frost, exist after the lapse of centuries, almost as fresh as if from the hand of the Moslem artist. I write in the midst of these mementoes of the past, in the fresh hour of early morning, in the fated Hall of the Abencerrages. The blood-stained fountain, the legendary monument of their massacre, is before me; the lofty jet almost casts its dew upon my paper. How difficult to reconcile the ancient tale of violence and blood with the gentle and peaceul scene around! Everything here appears calculated to inspire kind and happy feelings, for everything is delicate and beautiful. The very light falls tenderly from above, through the lantern of a

Plaster works and mocárabes (arch-shaped
ornaments) at the Court of the Lions.

dome tinted and wrought as if by fairy hands. Through the ample and fretted arch of the portal I behold the Court of Lions, with brilliant sunshine gleaming along its colonnades and sparkling in its fountains. The lively swallow dives into the court, and, rising with a surge, darts away twittering over the roofs; the busy bee toils humming among the flower-beds; and painted butterflies hover from plant to plant, and flutter up and sport with each other in the sunny air. It needs but a slight exertion of the fancy to picture some pensive beauty of the harem, loitering in these secluded haunts of Oriental luxury.

He, however, who would behold this scene under an aspect more in unison with its fortunes, let him come when the shadows of evening temper the brightness of the court, and throw a gloom into the surrounding halls. Then nothing can be more serenely melancholy, or more in harmony with the tale of departed grandeur.

At such times I am apt to seek the Hall of Justice, whose deep shadowy arcades extend across the upper end of the court. Here was performed, in presence of Ferdinand and Isabella and their triumphant court, the pompous ceremonial of high mass, on taking possession of the Alhambra. The very cross is still to be seen upon the wall, where the altar was erected, and where officiated the Grand Cardinal of Spain, and other of the highest religious dignitaries of the land. I picture to myself the scene when this place was filled with the conquering host, that mixture of mitred prelate and shaven monk, and steel-clad knight and silken courtier; when crosses and crosiers and religious standards were mingled with proud armorial-ensigns and the banners of the haughty chiefs of Spain, and flaunted in triumph through these Moslem halls. I picture to myself Columbus, the future discoverer of a world, taking his modest stand in a remote corner, the humble and neglected spectator of the pageant. I see in imagination the Catholic sovereigns prostrating themselves before the altar, and pouring forth thanks for their victory; while the

vaults resound with sacred minstrelsy, and the deep-toned **Te Deum.**

The transient illusion is over,—the pageant melts from the fancy,—monarch, priest, and warrior return into oblivion with the poor Moslems over whom they exulted. The hall of their triumph is waste and desolate. The bat flits about its twilight vault, and the owl hoots from the neighbouring tower of Comares.

Entering the Court of the Lions a few evenings since, I was almost startled at beholding a turbaned Moor quietly seated near the fountain. For a moment one of the fictions of the place seemed realised: an enchanted Moor had broken the spell of centuries, and become visible. He proved, however, to be a mere ordinary mortal: a native of Tetuan in Barbary, who had a shop in the Zacatin of Granada, where he sold rhubarb, trinkets, and perfumes. As he spoke Spanish fluently, I was enabled to hold conversation with him, and found him shrewd and intelligent. He told me that he came up the hill occasionally in the summer, to pass a part of the day in the Alhambra, which reminded him of the old palaces in Barbary, being built and adorned in similar style, though with more magnificence.

As we walked about the palace, he pointed out several of the Arabic inscriptions, as possessing much poetic beauty.

«Ah, **señor**», said he, «when the Moors held Granada, they were a gayer people than they are nowadays. They thought only of love, music, and poetry. They made stanzas upon every occasion, and set them all to music. He who could make the best verses, and she who had the most tuneful voice, might be sure of favour and preferment. In those days, if any one asked for bread, the reply was, make me a couplet; and the poorest beggar, if he begged in rhyme, would often be rewarded with a piece of gold».

«And is the popular feeling for poetry», said I, «entirely lost among you?»

«By no means, **señor;** the people of Barbary, even those of the lower classes, still make couplets, and good ones too, as in old times;

but talent is not rewarded as it was then; the rich prefer the jingle of their gold to the sound of poetry or music».

As he was talking, his eye caught one of the inscriptions which foretold perpetuity to the power and glory of the Moslem monarchs, the masters of this pile. He shook his head, and shrugged his shoulders, as he interpreted it. «Such might have been the case,» said he; «the Moslems might still have been reigning in the Alhambra, had not Boabdil been a traitor, and given up his capital to the Christians. The Spanish monarchs would never have been able to conquer it by open force.»

I endeavoured to vindicate the memory of the unlucky Boabdil from this aspersion, and to show that the dissensions which led to the downfall of the Moorish throne originated in the cruelty of his tiger-hearted father; but the Moor would admit of no palliation.

«Muley Abul Hassan,» said he, «might have been cruel; but he was brave, vigilant, and patriotic. Had he been properly seconded, Granada would still have been ours; but his son Boabdil thwarted his plans, crippled his power, sowed treason in his palace, and dissension in his camp. May the curse of God light upon him for his treachery!» With these words the Moor left the Alhambra.

The indignation of my turbaned companion agrees with an anecdote related by a friend, who, in the course of a tour in Barbary, had an interview with the Pacha of Tetuan. The Moorish governor was particular in his inquiries about Spain, and especially concerning the favoured region of Andalusia, the delights of Granada, and the remains of its royal palace. The replies awakened all those fond recollections, so deeply cherished by the Moors, of the power and splendour of their ancient empire in Spain. Turning to his Moslem attendants, the Pacha stroked his beard, and broke forth in passionate lamentations, that such a sceptre should have fallen from the sway of true believers. He consoled himself, however, with the persuasion, that the power and prosperity of the Spanish nation were on the

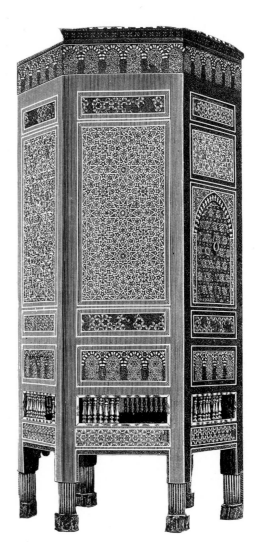

decline; that a time would come when the Moors would conquer their rightful domains; and that the day was perhaps not far distant when Mohammedan worship would again be offered up in the mosque of Cordova, and a Mohammedan prince sit on his throne in the Alhambra.

Such is the general aspiration and belief among the Moors of Barbary; who consider Spain, or Andaluz, as it was anciently called, their rightful heritage, of which they have been despoiled by treachery and violence. These ideas are fostered and perpetuated by the descendants of the exiled Moors of Granada, scattered among the cities of Barbary. Several of these reside in

Details of the white marble fountain at the Court of the Lions.

Night view of the Court of the Lions.

Tetuan, preserving their ancient names, such as Paez and Medina, and refraining from intermarriage with any families who cannot claim the same high origin. Their vaunted lineage is regarded with a degree of popular deference rarely shown in Mohammedan communities to any hereditary distinction, excepting in the royal line.

These families, it is said, continue to sigh after the terrestrial paradise of their ancestors, and to put up prayers in their mosques on Fridays, imploring Allah to hasten the time when Granada shall be restored to the faithful: an event to which they look forwards as fondly and confidently as did the Christian Crusaders to the recovery of the Holy Sepulchre. Nay, it is added, that some of them retain the ancient maps and deeds of the estates and gardens of their ancestors at Granada, and even the keys of the houses; holding them as evidences of their hereditary claims, to be produced at the anticipated day of restoration.

My conversation with the Moor set me to musing on the fate of Boabdil. Never was surname more applicable than that bestowed upon him by his subjects of el Zogoybi, or the Unlucky. His misfortunes began almost in his cradle, and ceased not even with his death. If ever he cherished the desire of leaving an honourable name on the historic page, how cruelly has he been defrauded of his hopes! Who is there that has turned the least attention to the romantic history of the Moorish domination in Spain, without kindling with indignation at the alleged atrocities of Boabdil? Who has not been touched with the woes of his lovely and gentle queen, subjected by him to a trial of life and death, on a false charge of infidelity? Who has not been shocked by his alleged murder of his sister and her two children, in a transport of passion? Who has not felt his blood boil at the inhuman massacre of the gallant Abencerrages, thirty-six of whom, it is affirmed, he ordered to be beheaded in the Court of Lions? All these charges have been reiterated in various forms; they have passed into ballads, dramas, and romances, until they

have taken too thorough possession of the public mind to be eradicated. There is not a foreigner of education that visits the Alhambra, but asks for the fountain where the Abencerrages were beheaded; and gazes with horror at the grated gallery where the queen is said to have been confined; not a peasant of the Vega or the Sierra, but sings the story in rude couplets, to the accompaniment of his guitar, while his hearers learn to execrate the very name of Boabdil.

Never, however, was name more foully and unjustly slandered. I have examined all the authentic chronicles and letters written by Spanish authors, contemporary with Boabdil; some of whom were in the confidence of the Catholic sovereigns, and actually present in the camp throughout the war. I have examined all the Arabian authorities I could get access to, through the medium of translation, and have found nothing to justify these dark and hateful accusations. The most of these tales may be traced to a work commonly called **The Civil Wars of Granada,** containing a pretended history of the feuds of the Zegries and Abencerrages, during the last struggle of the Moorish empire. The work appeared originally in Spanish, and professed to be translated from the Arabic by one Gines Perez de Hita, an inhabitant of Murcia. It has since passed into various languages, and Florian has taken from it much of the fable of his Gonsalvo of Cordova: it has thus, in a great measure, usurped the authority of real history, and is currently believed by the people, and especially the peasantry of Granada. The whole of it, however, is a mass of fiction, mingled with a few disfigured truths, which give it an air of veracity. It bears internal evidence of its falsity; the manners and customs of the Moors being extravagantly misrepresented in it, and scenes depicted totally incompatible with their habits and their faith, and which never could have been recorded by a Mohammedan writer. I confess there seems to me something almost criminal in the wilful perversions of this work: great latitude is undoubtedly to be allowed to

romantic fiction, but there are limits which it must not pass; and the names of the distinguished dead, which belong to history, are no more to be calumniated than those of the illustrious living. One would have thought, too, that the unfortunate Boabdil had suffered enough for his justifiable hostility to the Spaniards, by being stripped of his kingdom, without having his name thus wantonly traduced, and rendered a byword and a theme of infamy in his native land, and in the very mansion of his fathers!

Hall of the Two Sisters.

Dome in mocárabe style at the Sovereign Hall.

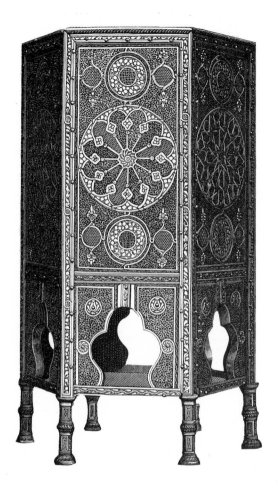

son with the scarves of herself and her female attendants during the darkness of the night to the hill-side, where some of his faithful adherents waited with fleet steeds to bear him to the mountains.

Between three and four hundred years have elapsed, yet this scene of the drama remains almost unchanged. As I paced the gallery, my imagination pictured the anxious queen leaning over the parapet, listening, with the throbbings of a mother's heart, to the last echoes of the horse's hoofs as her son scoured along the narrow valley of the Darro.

I next sought the gate by which Boabdil made his last exit from the Alhambra, when about to surrender his capital and kingdom. With the melancholy caprice of a broken spirit, or perhaps with some superstitious feeling, he requested of the Catholic monarchs that no one afterwards might be permitted to pass through it. His prayer, according to ancient chronicles, was complied with, through the sympathy of Isabella, and the gate was walled up.

I inquired for some time in vain for such a portal; at lenght my humble attendant, Mateo Ximenes, said it must be one closed up with stones, which, according to what he had heard from his father and grandfather, was the gateway by which King Chico had left the fortress. There was a mystery about it, and it had never been opened within the memory of the oldest inhabitant.

He conducted me to the spot. The gateway is in the centre of what was once an immense pile, called the Tower of the Seven Floors (**la Torre de los siete suelos**). It is famous in the neighbourhood as the scene of strange apparitions and Moorish enchantments. According to Swinburne the traveller, it was originally the great gate of entrance. The antiquaries of Granada pronounce it the entrance to that quarter of the royal residence where the king's bodyguards were stationed. It therefore might well form an immediate entrance and exit to the palace; while the grand Gate of Justice served as the entrance of state to the fortress. When Boabdil sallied by this gate to

MEMENTOES OF BOABDIL

While my mind was still warm with the subject of the unfortunate Boabdil, I set forth to trace the mementoes of him still existing in this scene of his sovereignty and misfortunes. In the tower of Comares, immediately under the Hall of Ambassadors, are two vaulted rooms, separated by a narrow passage; these are said to have been the prisons of himself and his mother, the virtuous Ayxa la Horra; indeed, no other part of the tower would have served for the purpose. The external walls of these chambers are of prodigious thickness, pierced with small windows secured by iron bars. A narrow stone gallery, with a low parapet, extends along three sides of the tower just below the windows, but at a considerable height from the ground. From this gallery, it is presumed, the queen lowered her descend to the Vega, where he was to surrender the keys of the city to the Spanish sovereigns, he left his vizier Aben Comixa to receive, at the gate of Justice, the detachment from the Christian army and the officers to whom the fortress was to be given up.

The once redoubtable Tower of the Seven Floors is now a mere wreck, having been blown up with gunpowder by the French, when they abandoned the fortress. Great masses of the wall lie scattered about, buried in luxuriant herbage, or overshadowed by vines and fig-trees. The arch of the gateway, though rent by the shock, still remains; but the last wish of poor Boabdil has again, though unintentionally, been fulfilled, for the portal has been closed up by loose stones gathered from the ruins, and remains impassable.

Mounting my horse, I followed up the route of the Moslem monarch from this place of his exit. Crossing the hill of Los Martyros, and keeping along the garden-wall of a convent bearing the same name, I descended a rugged ravine beset by thickets of aloes and Indian figs, and lined with caves and hovels swarming with gipsies. The descent was so steep and broken that I was fain to alight and lead my horse. By this **via dolorosa** poor Boabdil took his sad departure to avoid passing through the city; partly, perhaps, through unwillingness that its inhabitants should behold his humiliation; but chiefly, in all probability, lest it might cause some popular agitation. For the last reason, undoubtedly, the detachment sent to take possession of the fortress ascended by the same route.

Emerging from this rough ravine, so full of melancholy associations, and passing by the **puerta de los molinos** (the gate of the mills), I issued forth upon the public promenade called the Prado; and pursuing the course of the Xenil, arrived at a small chapel, once a mosque, now the Hermitage of San Sebastian. Here, according to tradition, Boabdil surrendered the keys of Granada to King Ferdinand. I rode slowly thence across the Vega to a village where the family and household of the unhappy king awaited him, for he had sent them forward on the preceding night from the Alhambra, that his mother and wife might not participate in his personal humiliation, or be exposed to the gaze of the conquerors. Following on in the route of the melancholy band of royal exiles, I arrived at the foot of a chain of barren and dreary heights, forming the skirt of the Alpuxarra Mountains. From the summit of one of these the unfortunate Boabdil took his last look at Granada; it bears a name expressive of his sorrows, **La Cuesta de las Lágrimas** (the hill of tears). Beyond it, a sandy road winds across a rugged cheerless waste, doubly dismal to the unhappy monarch, as it led to exile.

I spurred my horse to the summit of a rock, where Boabdil uttered his last sorrowful exclamation, as he turned his eyes from taking their farewell gaze: it is still denominated **el último suspiro del Moro** (the last sigh of the Moor). Who can wonder at his anguish at being expelled from such a kingdom and such an abode? With the Alhambra he seemed to be yielding up all the honours of his line, and all

Inner dome at the Hall of the Two Sisters.

Lindaraja Observatory.

the glories and delights of life.

It was here, too, that his affliction was embittered by the reproach of his mother, Ayxa, who had so often assisted him in times of peril, and had vainly sought to instil into him her own resolute spirit. «You do well», said she, «to weep as a woman over what you could ñot defend as a man;» a speech savouring more of the pride of the princess than the tenderness of the mother.

When this anecdote was related to Charles V., by Bishop Guevara, the emperor joined in the expression of scorn at the weakness of the wavering Boabdil. «Had I been he, or he been I,» said the haughty potentate, «I would rather have made this Alhambra my sepulchre than have lived without a kingdom in the Alpuxarra.» How easy it is for those in power and prosperity to preach heroism to the vanquished! how little can they understand that life itself may rise in value with the unfortunate when naught but life remains!

Slowly descending the «Hill of Tears,» I let my horse take his own loitering gait back to Granada, while I turned the story of the unfortunate Boabdil over in my mind.

In summing up the particulars, I found the balance inclining in his favour. Throughout the whole of his brief, turbulent, and disastrous reign, he gives evidencie of a mild and amiable character. He, in the first instance, won the hearts of his people by his affable and gracious manners; he was always placable, and never inflicted any severity of punishment upon those who occasionally rebelled against him. He was personally brave, but wanted moral courage; and, in times of difficulty and perplexity, was wavering and irresolute. This feebleness of spirit hastened his downfall, while it deprived him of that heroic grace which would have given grandeur and dignity to his fate, and rendered him worthy of closing the splendid drama of the Moslem domination in Spain.

LEGEND OF THE ROSE OF THE ALHAMBRA

For some time after the surrender of Granada by the Moors, that delightful city was a frequent and favourite residence of the Spanish sovereigns, until they were frightened away by successive shocks of earthquakes, which toppled down various houses, and made the old Moslem towers rock to their foundation.

Many, many years then rolled away, during which Granada was rarely honoured by a royal guest. The palaces of the nobility remained silent and shut up; and the Alhambra, like a slighted beauty, sat in mournful desolation among her neglected gardens. The tower of the **Infantas,** once the residence of the three beautiful Moorish princesses, partook of the general desolation; the spider spun her web athwart the gilded vault, and bats and owls nestled in those chambers that had been graced by the presence of Zayda, Zorayda, and Zorahayda. The neglect of this tower may have been partly owing to some superstitious notions of the neighbours. It was rumoured that the spirit of the youthful Zorahayda, who had perished in that tower, was often seen by moonlight seated beside the fountain in the hall, or moaning about the battlements, and that the notes of her silver lute would be heard at midnight by wayfarers passing along the glen.

At length the city of Granada was once more welcomed by the royal presence. All the world knows that Philip V. was the first Bourbon that swayed the Spanish sceptre. All the world knows that he married, in second nuptials, Elizabetta or Isabella (for they are the same), the beautiful princess of Parma; and all the world knows that by this chain of contingencies a French prince and an Italian princess were seated together on the Spanish throne. For a visit of this illustrious pair, the Alhambra was repaired and fitted up with all possible expedition. The arrival of the court changed the whole aspect of the lately deserted palace. The clangor of drum and trumpet, the tramp of steed about the avenues and outer court, the glitter of arms and display of banners about barbican and battlement, recalled the ancient and warlike glories of the fortress. A softer spirit, however, reigned within the royal palace. There was the rustling of robes and the cautious tread and murmuring voice of reverential courtiers about the ante-chambers; a loitering of pages and maids of honour about the gardens, and the sound of music stealing from open casements.

Among those who attended in the train of the monarchs was a favourite page of the queen, named **Ruyz de Alarcon.** To say that he was a favourite page of the queen was at once to speak his eulogium, for every one in the suite of the stately Elizabetta was chosen for grace, and beauty, and accomplishments. He was just turned of eighteen, light and lithe of form, and graceful as a young Antinous. To the queen he was all deference and respect, yet he was at heart a roguish stripling, petted and spoiled by the ladies about the court, and experienced in the ways of women far beyond his years.

This loitering page was one morning rambling about the groves of the Generalife, which overlook the grounds of the Alhambra. He had taken with him for his amusement a favourite ger-falcon of the queen. In the course of his rambles, seeing a bird rising from a thicket, he unhooded the hawk and let him fly. The falcon towered high in the air, made a swoop at his quarry, but missing it, soared away, regardless of the calls of the page. The latter followed the truant bird with his eye, in its capricious flight, until he saw it alight upon the battlements of a remote and lonely tower, in the outer wall of the Alhambra, built on the edge of a ravine that separated the royal fortress from the grounds of the Generalife. It was in fact the «Tower of the Princesses.»

The page descended into the ravine and approached the tower, but it had no entrance from the glen, and its lofty height rendered any attempt to scale it fruitless. Seeking one of the gates of the fortress, therefore, he made a wide circuit to that side of the tower facing within the walls.

A small garden, enclosed by a trellis-work of

Bathroom
Hall.

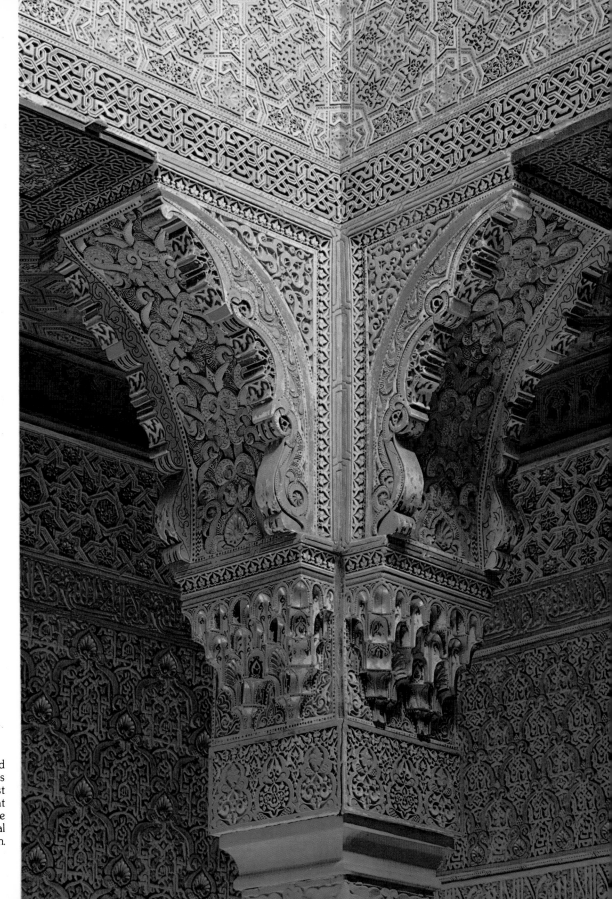

Polychromed
lattice works
of the Rest
Lounge at
the
Royal
Bathroom.

reeds overhung with myrtle, lay before the tower. Opening a wicket, the page passed between beds of flowers and thickets of roses to the door. It was closed and bolted. A crevice in the door gave him a peep into the interior. There was a small Moorish hall with fretted walls, light marble columns, and an alabaster fountain surrounded with flowers. In the centre hung a gilt cage containing a singing-bird; beneath it, on a chair, lay a tortoise-shell cat among reels of silk and other articles of female labour, and a guitar decorated with ribbons leaned against the fountain.

Ruyz de Alarcon was struck with these traces of female taste and elegance in a lonely, and, as he had supposed, deserted tower. They reminded him of the tales of enchanted halls current in the Alhambra; and the tortoise-shell cat might be some spell-bound princess.

He knocked gently at the door. A beautiful face peeped out from a little window above, but was instantly withdrawn. He waited, expecting that the door would be opened, but he waited in vain; no footstep was to be heard within— all was silent. Had his senses deceived him, or was this beautiful apparition the fairy of the tower? He knocked again, and more loudly. After a little while the beaming face once more peeped forth; it was that of a blooming damsel of fifteen. The page immediately doffed his plumed bonnet, and entreated in the most courteous accents to be permitted to ascend the tower in pursuit of his falcon.

«I dare not open the door, **Señor**», replied the little damsel, blushing, «my aunt has forbidden it.»

«I do beseech you, fair maid—it is the favourite falcon of the queen: I dare not return to the palace without it.»

«Are you then one of the cavaliers of the court?»

«I am, fair maid; but I shall lose the queen's favour and my place, if I lose this hawk.»

«**Santa Maria!** It is against you cavaliers of the court my aunt has charged me especially to bar the door.»

«Against wicked cavaliers doubtless, but I am

none of these, but a simple, harmless page, who will be ruined and undone if you deny me this small request».

The heart of the little damsel was touched by the distress of the page. It was a thousand pities he should be ruined for the want of so trifling a boon. Surely too he could not be one of those dangerous beings whom her aunt had described as species of cannibal, ever on the prowl to make prey of thoughtless damsels; he was gentle and modest, and stood so entreatingly with cap in hand, and looked so charming.

The sly page saw that the garrison began to waver, and redoubled his entreaties in such moving terms that it was not in the nature of mortal maiden to deny him; so the blushing little warden of the tower descended, and opened the door with a trembling hand, and if the page had been charmed by a mere glimpse of her countenance from the window, he was ravished by the full-length portrait now revealed to him. Her Andalusian bodice and trim **basquiña** set off the round but delicate symmetry of her form, which was as yet scarce verging into womanhood. Her glossy hair was parted on her forehead with scrupulous exactness, and decorated with a fresh-plucked rose, according to the universal custom of the country. It is true her complexion was tinged by the ardour of a southern sun, but it served to give richness to the mantling bloom of her cheek, and to heighten the lustre of her melting eyes.

Ruyz de Alarcon beheld all this with a single glance, for it became him not to tarry; he merely murmured his acknowledgments, and then bounded lightly up the spiral staircase in quest of his falcon.

He soon returned with the truant bird upon his fist. The damsel, in the meantime, had seated herself by the fountain in the hall, and was winding silk; but in her agitation she let fall the reel upon the pavement. The page sprang and picked it up, then dropping gracefully on one knee, presented it to her; but, seizing the hand extended to receive it, imprinted on it a kiss more fervent and devout than he had ever imprinted on the fair hand of his sovereign.

One of the beds in the Rest Hall.

Ceiling of the Rest Hall.

Inner dome of the Hall of the Abencerrajes.

Interior of the
Mihrab.

«Ava Maria Señor!» exclaimed the damsel, blushing still deeper with confusion and surprise, for never before had she received such a salutation.

The modest page made a thousand apologies, assuring her it was the way at court of expressing the most profound homage and respect.

Her anger, if anger she felt, was easily pacified, but her agitation and embarrassment continued, and she sat blushing deeper and deeper, with her eyes cast down upon her work, entangling the silk which she attempted to wind.

The cunning page saw the confusion in the opposite camp, and would fain have profited by it, but the fine speeches he would have uttered died upon his lips; his attempts at gallantry were awkward and ineffectual; and to his surprise, the adroit page, who had figured with such grace and effrontery among the most knowing and experienced ladies of the court, found himself awed and abashed in the presence of a simple damsel of fifteen.

In fact, the artless maiden, in her own modesty and innocence, had guardians more effectual than the bolts and bars prescribed by her vigilant aunt. Still, where is the female bosom proof against the first whisperings of love? The little damsel, with all her artlessness, instinctively comprehended all that the faltering tongue of the page failed to express, and her heart was fluttered at beholding, for the first time, a lover at her feet—and such a lover!

The diffidence of the page, though genuine, was short-lived, and he was recovering his usual ease and confidence, when a shrill voice was heard at a distance.

«My aunt is returning from mass!» cried the damsel in affright: «I pray you, **Señor**, depart».

«Not until you grant me that rose from your hair as a remembrance.

She hastily untwisted the rose from her raven locks. «Take it», cried she, agitated and blushing, «but pray begone».

The page took the rose, and at the same time covered with kisses the fair hand that gave it. Then, placing the flower in his bonnet, and taking the falcon upon his fist he bounded off through the garden, bearing away with him the heart of the gentle Jacinta.

When the vigilant aunt arrived at the tower, she remarked the agitation of her niece, and an air of confusion in the hall; but a word of explanation sufficed. «A ger-falcon had pursued his prey into the hall».

«Mercy on us! to think of a falcon flying into the tower. Did ever one hear of so saucy a hawk? Why, the very bird in the cage is not safe!»

The vigilant Fredegonda was one of the most wary of ancient spinsters. She had a becoming terror and distrust of what she denominated «the opposite sex», which had gradually increased through a long life of celibacy. Not that the good lady had ever suffered from their wiles, nature having set up a safeguard in her face that forbade all trespass upon her premises; but ladies who lave least cause to fear for themselves are most ready to keep a watch over their more tempting neighbours.

The niece was the orphan of an officer who had fallen in the wars. She had been educated in a convent, and had recently been transferred from her sacred asylum to the immediate guardianship of her aunt, under whose overshadowing care she vegetated in obscurity, like an opening rose blooming beneath a brier. Nor indeed is this comparison entirely accidental; for, to tell the truth, her fresh and dawning beauty had caught the public eye, even in her seclusion, and, with that poetical turn common to the people of Andalusia, the peasantry of the neighbourhood had given her the appellation of «the Rose of the Alhambra».

The wary aunt continued to keep a faithful watch over her tempting little niece as long as the court continued at Granada, and flattered herself that her vigilance had been successful. It is true the good lady was now and then discomposed by the tinkling of guitars and chanting of love-ditties from the moonlit groves beneath the tower; but she would exhort her niece to shut her ears against such idle minstrelsy, assuring her that it was one of the opposite sex, by which simple maids were often

lured to their undoing. Alas! what chance with a simple maid has a dry lecture against a moonlight serenade?

At length king Philip cut short his sojourn at Granada, and suddenly departed with all his train. The vigilant Fredegonda watched the royal pageant as it issued forth from the Gate of Justice, and descended the great avenue leading to the city. When the last banner disappeared from her sight, she returned exulting to her tower, for all her cares were over. To her surprise, a light Arabian steed pawed the ground at the wicket-gate of the garden;—to her horror she saw through the thickets of roses a youth in gaily embroidered dress, at the feet of her niece. At the sounds of her footsteps he gave a tender adieu, bounded lightly over the barrier of reeds and myrtles, sprang upon his horse, and was out of sight in an instant.

The tender Jacinta, in the agony of her grief, lost all thought of her aunt's displeasure. Throwing herself into her arms, she broke forth into sobs and tears.

«**Ay de mi!** cried she: «he's gone!—he's gone!—he's gone! and I shall never see him more!»

«Gone!—who is gone?—what youth is that I saw at your feet?»

«A queen's page, aunt, who came to bid me farewell».

«A queen's page, child!» echoed the vigilant Fredegonda, faintly, «and when did you become acquainted with the queen's page?»

«The morning that the ger-falcon came into the tower. It was the queen's ger-falcon, and he came in pursuit of it».

«Ah silly, silly girl! know that there are no ger-falcons half so dangerous as these young

Samples of polychromed tiles.

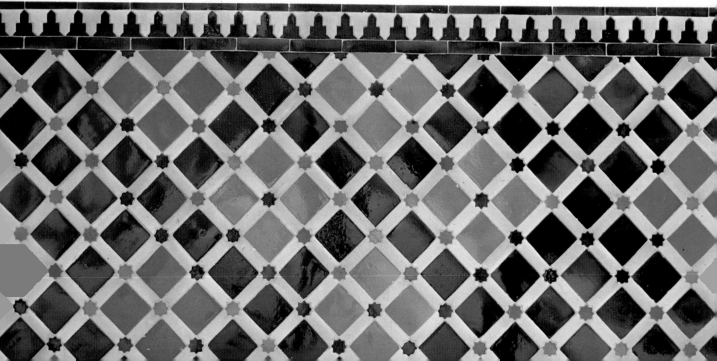

prankling pages, and it is precisely such simple birds as thee that they pounce upon».

The aunt was at first indignant at learning that in despite of her boasted vigilance, a tender intercourse had been carried on by the youthful lovers, almost beneath her eye; but when she found that her simple-hearted niece, though thus exposed, without the protection of bolt or bar, to all the machinations of the opposite sex, had come forth unsinged from the fiery ordeal, she consoled herself with the persuasion that it was owing to the chaste and cautious maxims in which she had, as it were, steeped her to the very lips.

While the aunt laid this soothing unction to her pride, the niece treasured up the oft-repeated vows of fidelity of the page. But what is the love of restless, roving man? A vagrant stream that dallies for a time with each flower upon its bank, then passes on, and leaves them all in tears. Days, weeks, months elapsed, and nothing more was heard of the page. The pomegranate ripened, the vine yielded up its fruit, the autumnal rains descended in torrents from the mountains; the Sierra Nevada became covered with a snowy mantle, and wintry blasts howled through the halls of the Alhambra—still he came not. The winter passed away. Again the genial spring burst forth with song and blossom and balmy zephyr; the snows melted from the mountains, until none remained but on the lofty summit of Nevada, glistening through the sultry summer air. Still nothing was heard of the forgetful page.

In the meantime the poor little Jacinta grew pale and thoughtful. Her former occupations and amusements were abandoned, her silk lay entangled, her guitar unstrung, her flowers were neglected, the notes of her bird unheeded, and her eyes, once so bright, were dimmed with secret weeping. If any solitude could be devised to foster the passion of a love-lorn damsel it would be such a place as the Alhambra, where everything seems disposed to produce tender and romantic reveries. It is a very paradise for lovers: how hard then to be alone in such a paradise—and not merely alone, but forsaken! «Alas, silly child!» would the staid and immaculate Fredegonda say, when she found her niece in one of her desponding moods—«did I not warn thee against the wiles and deceptions of these men? What couldst thou expect, too, from one of a haughty and aspiring family—thou an orphan, the descendant of a fallen and impoverished line? Be assured, if the youth were true, his father, who is one of the proudest nobles about the court, would prohibit his union with one so humble and portionless as thou. Pluck up thy resolution, therefore, and drive these idle notions from thy mind».

The words of the immaculate Fredegonda only served to increase the melancholy of her niece, but she sought to indulge it in private. At a late

Different views of the Alhambra.

The Partal Gardens.

hour one midsummer night, after her aunt had retired to rest, she remained alone in the hall of the tower, seated beside the alabaster fountain. It was here that the faithless page had first knelt and kissed her hand; it was here that he had often vowed eternal fidelity. The poor little damsel's heart was overladen with sad and tender recollections, her tears began to flow, and slowly fell drop by drop into the fountain. By degrees the crystal water became agitated, and—bubble—bubble—boiled up and was tossed about, until a female figure, richly clad in Moorish robes, slowly rose to view.

Jacinta was so frightened that she fled from the hall, and did not venture to return. The next morning she related what she had seen to her aunt, but the good lady treated it as a fantasy of her troubled mind, or supposed she had fallen asleep and dreamt beside the fountain. «Thou hast been thinking of the story of the three Moorish princesses that once inhabited this tower», continued she, «and it has entered into thy dreams».

«What story, aunt? I know nothing of it».

«Thou hast certainly hear of the three princesses, Zayda, Zorayda, and Zorahayda, who were confined in this tower by the king their father, and agreed to fly with three Christian cavaliers. The two first accomplished their escape, but the third failed in her resolution, and, it is said, died in this tower».

«I now recollect to have heard of it», said Jacinta, «and to have wept over the fate of the gentle Zorahayda».

«Thou mayest well weep over her fate», continued the aunt, «for the lover of Zorahayda was thy ancestor. He long bemoaned his Moorish love: but time cured him of his grief, and he married a Spanish lady, from whom thou art descended».

Jacinta ruminated upon these words. «That what I have seen is no fantasy of the brain», said she to herself, «I am confident. If indeed it be the spirit of the gentle Zorahayda, which I have heard lingers about this tower, of what should I be afraid? I'll watch by the fountain to-night—perhaps the visit will be repeated».

Towards midnight, when everything was quiet, she again took her seat in the hall. As the bell in the distant watchtower of the Alhambra struck the midnight hour, the fountain was again agitated; and bubble—bubble—bubble—it tossed about the waters until the Moorish female again rose to view. She was young and beautiful; her dress was rich with jewels, and in her hand she held a silver lute. Jacinta trembled and was faint, but was reassured by the soft and plaintive voice of the apparition, and the sweet expression of her pale, melancholy countenance.

«Daugther of mortality», said she, «what aileth thee? Why do thy tears trouble my fountain, and thy sighs and plaints disturb the quiet watches of the night?».

«I weep because of the faithlessness of man, and I bemoan my solitary and forsaken state».

«Take comfort; thy sorrows may yet have an end. Thou beholdest a Moorish princess, who, like thee, was unhappy in her love. A Christian knight, thy ancestor, won my heart, and would have borne me to his native land and to the bosom of his church. I was a convert in my heart, but I lacked courage equal to my faith, and lingered till too late. For this the evil genii are permitted to have power over me, and I remain enchanted in this tower until some pure Christian will deign to break the magic spell. Wilt thou undertake the task?».

«I will», replied the damsel, trembling.

«Come hither then, and fear not; dip thy hand in the fountain, sprinkle the water over me, and baptize me after the manner of thy faith; so shall the enchantment be dispelled, and my troubled spirit have repose».

The damsel advanced with faltering steps, dipped her hand in the fountain, collected water in the palm, and sprinkled it over the pale face of the phantom.

The latter smiled with ineffable benignity. She dropped her silver lute at the feet of Jacinta, crossed her white arms upon her bosom, and melted from sight, so that it seemed merely as if a shower of dewdrops had fallen into the fountain.

Jacinta retired from the hall filled with awe and wonder. She scarcely closed her eyes that night; but when she awoke at daybreak out of a troubled slumber, the whole appeared to her like a distempered dream. On descending into the hall, however, the truth of the vision was established, for beside the fountain she beheld the silver lute glittering in the morning sunshine. She hastened to her aunt, to relate all that had befallen her, and called her to behold the lute as a testimonial of the reality of her story. It the good lady had any lingering doubts, they were removed when Jacinta touched the instrument, for she drew forth such ravishing tones as to thaw even the frigid bosom of the immaculate Fredegonda, that region of eternal winter, into a genial flow. Nothing but supernatural melody could have produced such an effect.

The extraordinary power of the lute became every day more and more apparent. The wayfarer passing by the tower was detained, and, as it were, spell-bound in breathless ecstasy. The very birds gathered in the neighbouring trees, and hushing their own strains, listened in charmed silence.

Rumour soon spread the news abroad. The

Several views of the Partal Gardens.

The Tower of the Ladies at the Partal Gardens.

inhabitants of Granada thronged to the Alhambra to catch a few notes of the trascendent music that floated about the tower of Las Infantas.

The lovely little minstrel was at length drawn forth from her retreat. The rich and powerful of the land contended who should entertain and do honour to her; or rather, who should secure the charms of her lute to draw fashionable throngs to their saloons. Wherever she went her vigilant aunt kept a dragon watch at her elbow, awing the throngs of impassioned admirers who hung in raptures on her strains. The report of her wonderful powers spread from city to city. Malaga, Seville, Cordova, all became successively mad on the theme; nothing was talked of throughout Andalusia but the beautiful minstrel of the Alhambra. How could it be otherwise among a people so musical and gallant as the Andalusians, when the lute was

magical in its powers, and the minstrel inspired by love!

While all Andalusia was thus music mad, a different mood prevailed at the court of Spain. Philip V., as is well known, was a miserable hypochondriac, and subject to all kinds of fancies. Sometimes he would keep to his bed for weeks together, groaning under imaginary complaints. At other times he would insist upon abdicating his throne, to the great annoyance of his royal spouse, who had a strong relish for the splendours of a court and the glories of a crown, and guided the sceptre of her imbecile lord with an expert and steady hand.

Nothing was found to be so efficacious in dispelling the royal megrims as the power of music; the queen took care, therefore, to have the best performers, both vocal and instrumental, at hand, and retained the famous Italian singer Farinelli about the court as a kind

of royal physician.

At the moment we treat of, however, a freak had come over the mind of this sapient and illustrious Bourbon that surpassed all former vagaries. After a long spell of imaginary illness, which set all the strains of Farinelli and the consultations of a whole orchestra of court fiddlers at defiance, the monarch fairly, in idea, gave up the ghost, and considered himself absolutely dead.

This would have been harmless enough, and even convenient both to his queen and courtiers, had he been content to remain in the quietude befitting a dead man; but to their annoyance he insisted upon having the funeral ceremonies performed over him, and, to their inexpressible perplexity, began to grow impatient, and to revile bitterly at them for negligence and disrespect, in leaving him unburied. What was to be done? To disobey the king's positive commands was monstruous in the eyes of the obsequious courtiers of a punctilious court—but to obey him, and bury him alive would be downright regicide!

In the midst of this fearful dilemma a rumour reached the court of the female minstrel who was turning the brains of all Andalusia. The queen despatched missions in all haste to summon her to St. Ildefonso, where the court at that time resided.

Within a few days, as the queen with her maids of honour was walking in those stately gardens, intended, with their avenues and terraces and fountains, to eclipse the glories of Versailles, the far-famed minstrel was conducted into her presence. The imperial Elizabetta gazed with surprise at the youthful and unpretending appearance of the little being that had set the world madding. She was in her picturesque Andalusian dress, her silver lute in hand, and stood with modest and downcast eyes, but with a simplicity and freshness of beauty that still bespoke her «the Rose of the Alhambra.»

As usual she was accompanied by the ever-vigilant Fredegonda, who gave the whole history of her parentage and descent to the inquiring queen. If the stately Elizabetta had been

interested by the appearance of Jacinta, she was still more pleased when she learnt that she was of a meritorious though impoverished line, and that her father had bravely fallen in the service of the crown. «If thy powers equal thy renown,» said she, «and thou canst cast forth this evil spirit that possesses thy sovereign, thy fortunes shall henceforth be my care, and honours and wealth attend thee.»

Impatient to make trial of her skill, she led the way at once to the apartment of the moody monarch.

Jacinta followed with downcast eyes through

Court of the
Acequia
(irrigation
channel) at the
Generalife.

Entrance of the Court of the Acequia.

files of guards and crowds of courtiers. They arrived at length at a great chamber hung with black. The windows were closed to exclude the light of day: a number of yellow wax tapers in silver sconces diffused a lugubrious light, and dimly revealed the figures of mutes in mourning dresses, and courtiers who glided about with noiseless step and woe-begone visage. In the midst of a funeral bed or bier, his hands folded on his breast, and the tip of his nose just visible, lay extended this would-be-buried monarch.

The queen entered the chamber in silence, and pointing to a footstool in an obscure corner, beckoned to Jacinta to sit down and commence. At first she touched her lute with a faltering hand, but gathering confidence and animation as she proceeded, drew forth such soft aërial harmony, that all present could scarce believe it mortal. As to the monarch, who had already considered himself in the world of spirits, he set it down for some angelic melody or the music of the sphere. By degrees the theme was varied, and the voice of the minstrel accompanied the instrument. She poured forth one of the legendary ballads treating of the ancient glories of the Alhambra and the achievements of the Moors. Her whole soul entered into the theme, for with the recollections of the Alhambra was associated the story of her love. The funeral-chamber resounded with the animating strain. It entered into the gloomy heart of the monarch. He raised his head and gazed around: he sat up on his couch, his eye began to kindle—at length, leaping upon the floor, he called for sword and buckler.

The triumph of music, or rather of the enchanted lute, was complete; the demon of melancholy was cast forth; and, as it were, a dead man brought to life. The windows of the apartment were thrown open; the glorious effulgence of Spanish sunshine burst into the late lugubrious chamber; all eyes sought the lovely enchantress, but the lute had fallen from her hand, she had sunk upon the earth, and the next moment was clasped to the bosom of Ruyz de Alarcon.

The nuptials of the happy couple were celebrated soon afterwards with great splendour, and «the Rose of the Alhambra» became the ornament and delight of the court. «But hold—not so fast»—I hear the reader exclaim; «this is jumping to the end of a story at a furious rate! First let us know how Ruyz de Alarcon managed to account to Jacinta for his long neglect?» Nothing more easy; the venerable, time-honoured excuse, the opposition to his wishes by a proud, pragmatical old father: besides, young people who really like one another soon come to an amicable understanding, and bury all past grievances when once they meet.

But how was the proud, pragmatical old father reconciled to the match?

Oh! as to that, his scruples were easily overcome by a word or two from the queen; especially as dignities and rewards were showered upon the blooming favourite of royalty. Besides, the lute of Jacinta, you know, possessed a magic power, and could control the most stubborn head and hardest breast.

And what came of the enchanted lute?

Oh, that is the most curious matter of all, and plainly proves the truth of the whole story. That lute remained for some time in the family, but was purloined and carried off, as was supposed, by the great singer Farinelli, in pure jealousy. At his death it passed into other hands in Italy, who were ignorant of its mystic powers, and melting down the silver, transferred the strings to an old Cremona fiddle. The strings still retain something of their magic virtues. A word in the reader's ear, but let it go no further: that fiddle is now bewitching the whole world,—it is the fiddle of Paganini!

THE GOVERNOR AND THE NOTARY

In former times there ruled, as governor of the Alhambra, a doughty old cavalier, who, from having lost one arm in the wars, was commonly known by the name of **el Gobernador Manco,** or «the one-armed governor». He in fact prided himself upon being an old soldier, wore his

The gardens of the Generalife.

The gardens of
the Generalife

moustaches curled up to his eyes, a pair of campaigning boots, and a toledo as long as a spit, with his pocket-handkerchief in the basket-hilt.

He was, moreover, exceedingly proud and punctilious, and tenacious of all his privileges and dignities. Under his sway the immunities of the Alhambra, as a royal residence and domain, where rigidly exacted. No one was permitted to enter the fortress with fire-arms, or even with a sword or staff, unless he were of a certain rank; and every horseman was obliged to dismount at the gate, and lead his horse by the bridle. Now as the hill of the Alhambra rises from the very midst of the city of Granada, being, as it were, an excrescence of the capital, it must at all times be somewhat irksome to the captain-general, who commands the province, to thus have an **imperium in imperio,** a petty independent post in the very centre of his domains. It was rendered the more galling, in the present instance, from the irritable jealousy of the old governor, that took fire on the least question of authority and jurisdiction; and from the loose vagrant character of the people who had gradually nestled themselves within the fortress, as in a sanctuary, and thence carried on a system of roguery and depredation at the expense of the honest inhabitants of the city. Thus there was a perpetual feud and heart-burning between the captain-general and the governor, the more virulent on the part of the latter, inasmuch as the smallest of two neighbouring potentates is always the most captious about his dignity. The stately palace of the captain-general stood in the Plaza Nueva, immediately at the foot of the hill of the Alhambra; and here was always a bustle and parade of guards, and domestics, and city functionaries. A beetling bastion of the fortress overlooked the palace and public square in front of it; and on this bastion the old governor would occasionally strut backwards and forwards, with his toledo girded by his side, keeping a wary eye down upon his rival, like a hawk reconnoitring his quarry from his nest in a dry tree.

Whenever he descended into the city, it was in grand parade; on horseback, surrounded by his guards; or in his state coach, an ancient and unwieldy Spanish edifice of carved timber and gilt leather, drawn by eight mules, with running footmen, outriders, and lackeys; on which occasions he flattered himself he impressed every beholder with awe and admiration as vicegerent of the king; though the wits of Granada, particulary those who loitered about the palace of the captain-general, were apt to sneer at his petty parade, and, in allusion to the vagrant character of his subjects, to greet him with the appellation of «the king of the beggars». One of the most fruitful sources of dispute between these two doughty rivals was the right claimed by the governor to have all things passed free of duty through the city that were intended for the use of himself or his garrison. By degrees this privilege had given rise to extensive smuggling. A nest of **contrabandistas** took up their abode in the hovels of the fortress and the numerous caves in its vicinity, and drove a thriving business under the connivance of the soldiers of the garrison.

The vigilance of the captain-general was aroused. He consulted his legal adviser and factotum, a shrewd meddlesome **escribano,** or notary, who rejoiced in an opportunity of perplexing the old potentate of the Alhambra, and involving him in a maze of legal subtleties. He advised the captain-general to insist upon the right of examining every convoy passing through the gates of this city, and penned a long letter for him in vindication of the right. Governor Manco was a straightforward cut-and-thrust old soldier, who hated an **escribano** worse than the devil, and this one in particular worse than all other **escribanos.**

«What!» said he, curling up his moustaches fiercely, «does the captain-general set his man of the pen to practise confusions upon me? I'll let him see an old soldier is not to be baffled by schoolcraft.»

He seized his pen and scrawled a short letter in a crabbed hand, in which, without deigning to enter into argument, he insisted on the right of transit free of search, and denounced vengeance on any custom-house officer who should lay his unhallowed hand on any convoy protected by the flag of the Alhambra. While this question was agitated between the two pragmatical potentates, it so happened that a mule laden with supplies for the fortress arrived one day at the gate of Xenil, by which it was to traverse a suburb of the city on its way to the Alhambra. The convoy was headed by a testy old corporal, who had long served under the governor, and was a man after his own heart; as rusty and staunch as an old toledo blade.

As they approached the gate of the city, the corporal placed the banner of the Alhambra on the pack-saddle of the mule, and drawing himself up to a perfect perpendicular, advanced with his head dressed to the front, but with the wary side-glance of a cur passing through hostile ground and ready for a snap and a snarl.

«Who goes there?» said the sentinel at the gate.

«Soldier of the Alhambra!» said the corporal, without turning his head.

«What have you in charge?»

«Provisions for the garrison.»

«Proceed.»

The corporal marched straight forward, followed by the convoy, but had not advanced many paces before a posse of custom-house officers rushed out of a small toll-house.

«Hallo there!» cried the leader. «Muleteer, halt, and open those packages.»

The corporal wheeled round and drew himself up in battle array. «Respect the flag of the Alhambra,» said he; «these things are for the governor.»

«A **figo** for the governor and a **figo** for his flag. Muleteer, halt, I say.»

«Stop the convoy at your peril!» cried the corporal, cocking his musket. «Muleteer, proceed.»

The muleteer gave his beast a hearty thwack; the custom-house officer sprang forward and seized the halter; whereupon the corporal levelled his piece and shot him dead.

The street was immediately in an uproar. The old corporal was seized, and after undergoing sundry kicks, and cuffs, and cudgellings, which are generally given impromptu by the mob in Spain as a foretaste of the after penalties of the law, he was loaded with irons and conducted to the city prison, while his comrades were permitted to proceed with the convoy, after it had been well rummaged, to the Alhambra.

The old governor was in a towering passion when he heard of this insult to his flag and capture of his corporal. For a time he stormed about the Moorish halls, and vapoured about the bastions, and looked down fire and sword upon the palace of the captain-general. Having vented the first ebullition of his wrath, he despatched a message demanding the surrender of the corporal, as to him alone belonged the right of sitting in judgment on the offences of those under his command. The captain-general,

Building and reliefs of the Palace of Carlos V at the Alhambra.

Building and reliefs of the Palace of Carlos V at the Alhambra.

aided by the pen of the delighted **escribano,** replied at great length, arguing, that, as the offence had been commited within the walls of his city, and against one of his civil officers, it was clearly within his proper jurisdiction. The governor rejoined by a repetition of his demand; the captain-general gave a sur-rejoinder of still greater length and legal acumen; the governor became hotter and more peremptory in his demands, and the captain-general cooler and more copious in his replies; until the old lion-hearted soldier absolutely roared with fury at being thus entangled in the meshes of legal controversy.

While the subtle **escribano** was thus amusing himself at the expense of the governor, he was conducting the trial of the corporal, who, mewed up in a narrow dungeon of the prison, had merely a small grated window at which to show his iron-bound visage and receive the consolations of his friends.

A mountain of written testimony was diligently heaped up, according to Spanish form, by the indefatigable **escribano;** the corporal was completely overwhelmed by it. He was convicted of murder, and sentenced to be hanged.

It was in vain the governor sent down remonstrance and menace from the Alhambra. The fatal day was at hand, and the corporal was put **in capilla,** that is to say, in the chapel of the prison, as is always done with culprits the day before execution, that they may meditate on their approaching end and repent them of their sins.

Seeing things drawing to extremity, the old governor determined to attend to the affair in person. For this purpose he ordered out his carriage of state, and, surrounded by his guards, rumbled down the avenue of the Alhambra into the city. Driving to the house of the **escribano,** he summoned him to the portal.

The eye of the old governor gleamed like a coal at beholding the smirking man of the law advancing with an air of exultation.

«What is this I hear,» cried he, «that you are about to put to death one of my soldiers?»

«All according to law—all in strict form of justice,» said the self-sufficient **escribano,** chuckling and rubbing his hands; «I can show your Excellency the written testimony in the case.»

«Fetch it hither», said the governor. The **escribano** bustled into his office, delighted with having another opportunity of displaying his ingenuity at the expense of the hard-headed veteran. He returned with a satchel full of papers, and began to read a long deposition with professional volubility. By this time a crowd had collected, listening with outstretched necks and gaping mouths.

«Prithee, man, get into the carriage, out of this pestilent throng, that I may the better hear thee,» said the governor.

The **escribano** entered the carriage, when, in a twinkling, the door was closed, the coachman smacked his whip,—mules, carriage, guards, and all dashed off at a thundering rate, leaving the crowd in gaping wonderment; nor did the governor pause until he had lodged his prey in once of the strongest dungeons of the Alhambra.

He then sent down a flag of truce in military style, proposing a cartel, or exchange of prisioners,—the corporal for the notary. The pride of the captain-general was piqued; he returned a contemptuous refusal, and forthwith caused a gallows, tall and strong, to be erected in the centre of the Plaza Nueva for the execution of the corporal.

«Oho! is that the game?» said Governor Manco. He gave orders, and immediately a gibbet was reared on the verge of great beetling bastion that overlooked the Plaza. «Now,» said he, in a message to the captain-general, «hang my soldier when you please; but at the same time that he is swung off in the square, look up to see your **escribano** dangling against the sky.»

The captain general was inflexible; troops were paraded in the square; the drums beat, the bell tolled. An immense multitude of amateurs gathered together to behold the execution. On the other hand, the governor paraded his garrison on the bastion, and tolled the funeral dirge of the notary from the **Torre de la Campana,** or Tower of the Bell.

The notary's wife pressed through the crowd, with a whole progeny of little embryo **escribanos** at her heels, and throwing herself at the feet of the captain-general, implored him not to sacrifice the life of her husband, and the welfare of herself and her numerous little ones, to a point of pride; «for you know the old governor too well,» said she, «to doubt that he will put his threat in execution, if you hang the soldier.»

The captain-general was overpowered by her

Court at the Palace of Carlos V.

Sunset at the Alhambra.

tears and lamentations, and the clamours of her callow brood. The corporal was sent up to the Alhambra, under a guard, in his gallows garb, like a hooded friar, but with head erect and a face of iron. The **escribano** was demanded in exchange, according to the cartel. The once bustling and self-sufficient man of the law was drawn forth from his dungeon more dead than alive. All his flippancy and conceit had evaporated; his hair, it is said, had nearly turned gray with affright, and he had a downcast, dogged look, as if he still felt the halter round his neck.

The old governor stuck his one arm akimbo, and for a moment surveyed him with an iron smile. «Henceforth, my friend,» said he, «moderate your zeal in hurrying others to the gallows; be not too certain of your safety, even though you should have the law on your side; and above all, take care how you play off your schoolcraft another time upon an old soldier.»

THE AUTHOR'S FAREWELL TO GRANADA

My serene and happy reign in the Alhambra was suddenly brought to a close by letters which reached me, while indulging in oriental luxury in the cool hall of the baths, summoning me away from my Moslem elysium, to mingle once more in the bustle and business of the dusty world. How was I to encounter its toils and turmoils, after such a life of repose and reverie! How was I to endure its commonplace, after the poetry of the Alhambra!

But little preparation was necessary for my departure. A two-wheeled vehicle, called a **tartana,** very much resembling a covered cart, was to be the travelling equipage of a young Englishman and myself through Murcia, to Alicant and Valencia, on our way to France; and a long-limbed varlet, who had been a **contrabandista,** and, for aught I knew, a robber, was to be our guide and guard. The preparations were soon made, but the departure was the difficulty. Day after day was it postponed; day after day was spent in lingering

about my favourite haunts, and day after day they appeared more delightful in my eyes. The social and domestic little world also, in which I had been moving, had become singularly endeared to me; and the concern evinced by them at my intended departure, convinced me that my kind feelings were reciprocated. Indeed, when at length the day arrived, I did not dare venture upon a leavetaking at the good dame Antonia's; I saw the soft heart of little Dolores, at least, was brim full and ready for an overflow. So I bade a silent adieu to the palace and its inmates, and descended into the city as if intending to return. There, however, the **tartana** and the guide were ready; so, after taking a noon-day's repast with my fellow-traveller at the **Posada,** I set out with him on our journey.

Humble was the cortège and melancholy the departure of **El Rey Chico** the Second! Manuel, the nephew of **Tia Antonia,** Mateo, my officious but now disconsolate squire, and two or three old invalids of the Alhambra with whom I had grown into gossiping companionship, had come down to see me off; for it is one of the good old customs of Spain to sally forth several miles to meet a coming friend, and to accompany him as far on his departure. Thus then we set out, our long-legged guard striding ahead, with his **escopeta** on his shoulder; Manuel and Mateo on each side of the **tartana,** and the old invalids behind.

At some little distance to the north of Granada, the road gradually ascends the hills; here I alighted and walked up slowly with Manuel, who took this occasion to confide to me the secret of his heart and of all those tender concerns between himself and Dolores, with which I had been already informed by the all-knowing and all-revealing Mateo Ximenes. His doctor's diploma had prepared the way for their union, and nothing more was wanting but the dispensation of the Pope, on account of their consanguinity. Then, if he could get the post of Medico of the fortress his happiness would be complete! I congratulated him on the judgment and good taste he had shown in his choice of a helpmate; invoked all possible felicity on their union, and trusted that the abundant affections of the kind-hearted little Dolores would in time have more stable objects to occupy them than recreant cats and truant pigeons.

It was indeed a sorrowful parting when I took leave of these good people and saw them slowly descend the hills; now and then round to wave me a last adieu. Manuel, it is true, had cheerful prospects to console him, but poor Mateo seemed perfectly cast down. It was to him a grievous fall from the station of prime minister and historiographer, to his old brown cloak and his starveling mystery of ribbon-weaving; and the poor devil, notwithstanding his occasional officiousness, had, somehow or other, acquired a stronger hold on my sympathies than I was aware of. It would have really been a consolation in parting, could I have anticipated the good fortune in store for him, and to which I had contributed; for the importance I had appeared to give to his tales and gossip and local knowledge, and the frequent companionship in which I had indulged him in the course of my strolls, had elevated his idea of his own qualifications and opened a new career to him; and the son of the Alhambra has since become its regular and well-paid cicerone; insomuch that I am told he has never been obliged to resume the ragged old brown cloak in which I first found him.

Towards sunset I came to where the road wound into the mountains, and here I paused to take a last look at Granada. The hill on which I stood commanded a glorious view of the city, the Vega, and the surrounding mountains. It was at an opposite point of the compass from **La cuesta de las lágrimas** (the hill of tears) noted for the «last sigh of the Moor». I now could realize something of the feelings of poor Boabdil when he bade adieu to the paradise he was leaving behind, and beheld before him a rugged and sterile road conducting him to exile. The setting sun as usual shed a melancholy effulgence on the ruddy towers of the Alhambra. I could faintly discern the balconied window of the tower of Comares, where I had indulged in so many delightful reveries. The bosky groves and gardens about the city were richly gilded with the sunshine, the purple haze of a summer evening was gathering over the Vega; everything was lovely, but tenderly and sadly so, to my parting gaze.

«I will hasten from this prospect», thought I, «before the sun is set. I will carry away a recollection of it clothed in all its beauty».

With these thoughts I pursued my way among the mountains. A little further and Granada, the Vega and the Alhambra, were shut from my view: and thus ended one of the pleasantest dreams of a life, which the reader perhaps may think has been but too much made up of dreams.

INDEX

PALACE OF THE ALHAMBRA   6
THE HALL OF AMBASSADORS   22
THE MYSTERIOUS CHAMBERS   30
THE COURT OF LIONS   42
MEMENTOES OF BOABDIL   54
LEGEND OF THE ROSE OF
THE ALHAMBRA   59
THE GOVERNOR AND
THE NOTARY   82
THE AUTHOR'S FAREWELL
TO GRANADA   94

Printed in Spain  GEOCOLOR®

SIRVENSAE Av. J. Antonio, 754 - BARCELONA Dep. Legal B. 14561-79